EQUESTRIAN SPORTS IN THE UNITED KINGDOM

Books LLC®, Wiki Series, Memphis, USA, 2011. ISBN: 9781157431381. www.booksllc.net
Copyright: http://creativecommons.org/licenses/by-sa/3.0/deed.en

Table of Contents

British equestrians
Alec Scott 2
Alexandra Tolstoy 2
Andrew Ducrow 3
Anne, Princess Royal 3
Arthur Rook 7
Ben Maher 7
Bertie Hill 8
Brian Turner Tom Lawrence 8
Bridget Parker (equestrian) 8
Caroline Pratt 8
Christopher Bartle 9
Daisy Dick 10
Derek Allhusen 10
Douglas Stewart (equestrian) 10
Edward Howard-Vyse 11
Edward Radcliffe-Nash 11
Ellen Whitaker 12
Elwyn Hartley Edwards 12
Emma Hindle 12
Flora Harris 13
Francis Weldon 13
Geoff Billington 13
Harry Llewellyn 14
Harvey Smith (equestrian) 14
Helen Preece 15
Herbert Scott (equestrian) 15
Jane Gregory 15

Jane Holderness-Roddam 16
Jeanette Brakewell 16
Joanne Eccles 16
John Saint Ryan 16
John Whitaker (equestrian) 16
Kristina Cook 17
Laura Bechtolsheimer 17
Leslie Law 17
Lizzie Purbrick 18
Louise Skelton 18
Lucinda Green 18
Madeleine Gurdon 19
Marion Rose Halpenny 20
Mark Armstrong (equestrian) 20
Mark Phillips 20
Mary Gordon-Watson 21
Mary King (equestrian) 21
Michael Whitaker 24
Nick Skelton 25
Norman Arthur 26
Oliver Skeete 26
Pat Smythe 27
Paul Aloysius Kenna 28
Pippa Funnell 28
Polly Stockton 30
R. S. Summerhays 30
Richard Fanshawe (equestrian) 30
Richard Walker (equestrian) 30

Sarah Piercy 31
Sheila Willcox 31
Tim Stockdale 31
Timothy Grubb 31
Virginia Leng 32
Wilfred White (equestrian) 32
William Fox-Pitt 32
William Funnell 34
Zara Phillips 34

Equestrian sports in the United Kingdom
All England Jumping Course at Hickstead 35
Badminton Horse Trials 37
Blenheim Horse Trials 39
Bramham Horse Trials 39
Burghley Horse Trials 40
Olympia London International Horse Show 41
Royal Windsor Horse Show 41
Tent pegging 41

Royal International Horse Show
2010 Longines Royal International Horse Show 42
Royal International Horse Show 43

Introduction

Purchase of this book entitles you to a free trial membership in the publisher's book club at www.booksllc.net. (Time limited offer.) Simply enter the barcode number from the back cover onto the membership form. The book club entitles you to select from hundreds of thousands of books at no additional charge. You can also download a digital copy of this and related books to read on the go. Simply enter the title or subject onto the search form to find them.

Each chapter in this book ends with a URL to a hyperlinked online version. Type the URL exactly as it appears. If you change the URL's capitalization it won't work. Use the online version to access related pages, websites, footnotes, tables, color photos, updates. Click the version history tab to see the chapter's contributors. Click the edit link to suggest changes.

A large and diverse editor base collaboratively wrote the book, not a single author. After a long process of discussion and debate, the chapters gradually took on a neutral point of view reached through consensus. Additional editors expanded and contributed to chapters striving to achieve balance and comprehensive coverage. This reduced the regional or cultural bias found in many other books and provided access and breadth on subject matter otherwise little documented.

Alec Scott

Alexander "Alec" Brassey Jonathan Scott (October 16, 1906 – June 11, 1978) was a British horse rider who competed in the 1936 Summer Olympics.

In 1936 he and his horse *Bob Clive* won the bronze medal as part of the British eventing team, after finishing seventh in the individual eventing competition.

Source (edited): "http://en.wikipedia.org/wiki/Alec_Scott"

Alexandra Tolstoy

Alexandra Tolstoy FRGS (born **Alexandra Tolstoy-Miloslavsky**, 1974; married name **Alexandra Galimzyanova**) is an equine adventurer, broadcaster and businesswoman, a fellow of the Royal Geographical Society. She has made several long distance journeys on horses which have provided the material for television documentaries, books and talks.

The filming of *Horse People with Alexandra Tolstoy*, a television series for the BBC filmed in 2008, was reported to have contributed to the breakdown of her marriage in 2009.

Life

The daughter of Nikolai Tolstoy, Tolstoy studied for a Master of Arts degree in Russian at Edinburgh University which enabled her to spend a year in Russia. In 2003, she wrote of Edinburgh that -
It's where I made some of my closest friends and enjoyed four very happy and carefree years... Edinburgh has drinking hours that are the envy of all other British universities. Our only worry was how to fill the time between 4am and 6am, when the pubs were shut... The seeds were sown there for the great passions in my life.

She next moved to London, joining Credit Suisse First Boston's graduate scheme as a Eastern European Equities broker. She resigned after a year and spent the next two years working and traveling abroad during which time she spent six weeks walking the old Camino de Santiago pilgrimage route through Spain.

In 1999, she was part of a team which spent eight months travelling by horse and camel along a 5,000-mile length of the Silk Road. One of the support team members, an Uzbek show jumper, Shamil Galimzyanov, was to become her future husband. Upon completing the expedition, she moved to Moscow to complete her account of the expedition, *The Last Secrets of the Silk Road*, and to continue travelling in central Asia.

In 2000 Tolstoy and a friend rode 3,000 miles on horseback through Mongolia and Siberia.

In September 2003 Tolstoy and Galimzyanov were married in the Russian Orthodox Cathedral in Bayswater, London, after which they set up their home in a small Moscow apartment.

In 2004, along with her husband, she embarked upon the 2,700 mile journey from Turkmenistan to Moscow, retracing an expedition undertaken by twenty-eight Turkmen riders in 1935, who took 84 days to cover the distance. Riding Akhal-Teke horses, they were stopped from completing the journey by an outbreak of foot-and-mouth disease, resuming it in 2006 arriving in Moscow in November.

While living in Moscow, Tolstoy is reported to have taught English to the families of several 'oligarchs' and to have befriended the ex-billionaire Sergei Pugachyov.

When not travelling on her own expeditions, Tolstoy continues to write, organise riding holidays in Central Asia, work as an interior designer and for BDI, a brand development company assisting European companies to develop their business in the countries of the former Soviet Union.

In 2008, she spent a month filming *Horse People with Alexandra Tolstoy*, a television series for BBC Television in which she visited five quite different communities working with horses around the world. The BBC objected to her husband accompanying her, and this was later reported to have tested the marriage, which broke down in 2009 shortly after the birth of a baby boy. Tolstoy decided not to return to her former home in Moscow and in April 2009 she established herself with her son at a house in Chelsea. In June 2009, she was reported to have engaged "highly paid lawyers" to protect her private life.

In the summer of 2009, Tolstoy was reported to be staying in the South of France at a villa with Sergueï Pugachev and also to be helping him to find a country estate in England. In December she acquired a farmhouse near Malvern in Herefordshire for herself. Her distant cousin Alexander Nekrassov has stated that Pugachev is the father of Tolstoy's son. A second son Ivan was born in June 2010.

The BBC hopes for more television work, with a spokesman commenting "Alexandra's Horse People was very popular and she could well do more". Tolstoy was reported in 2009 to be considering making a series about high society in contemporary Russia.

Filmography

- *Horse People with Alexandra Tolstoy*

Source (edited): "http://en.wikipedia.org/wiki/Alexandra_Tolstoy"

Andrew Ducrow

Andrew Ducrow (1793–1842) was a British circus performer, often called the "Father of British circus equestrianism" and "the Colossus of equestrians" he was the originator of horsemanship acts and proprietor of the Astley's Amphitheatre. Ducrow was trained by his father who had immigrated to England from Belgium in 1793. The "Courier of St. Petersburg", his most famous act, was the forerunner to modern horse acts and is still performed today at equestrian events.

Ducrow performed within the United Kingdom and in Europe, including in famous venues such as Convent Garden and Drury Lane. He is most famous as the proprietor of Astley's Amphitheatre, where he was also the chief performer. Referred to by some as "the Chippendales of his day," Ducrow and his sons would dress in "fleshings" (flesh-coloured body stockings) and would perform physique poses posed as plastiques while standing upon the rumps of white stallions which could carry them round the amphitheatre several times.

Pablo Fanque, the black circus equestrian and later circus owner, best known from his mention in The Beatles song "Being for the Benefit of Mr. Kite!" on the album Sgt. Pepper's Lonely Hearts Club Band, worked in Ducrow's circus for some time.

Ducrow's shows proved immensely popular. Unfortunately, the Astley's Amphitheatre succumb three times to fire. After the third time in 1841, Ducrow collapsed from a mental breakdown and died shortly thereafter in 1842. William Batty took over management of Astley's Amphitheatre.

Ducrow is buried on the Main (or Centre) Avenue at Kensal Green Cemetery in London, England near the tomb of the Duke of Sussex, one of the most desirable burial plots of the time. His tomb is one of the largest and most decorated tombs within the cemetery. The decoration is primarily pagan, being drawn from Greek and Egyptian sources. There is no Christian-inspired decoration. The tomb was designed by Ducrow's theatrical designer and originally was brightly painted in pastel hues to attract the eye. These have faded over time.

Mausoleum for Andrew Ducrow in Kensal Green Cemetery, London

Source (edited): "http://en.wikipedia.org/wiki/Andrew_Ducrow"

Anne, Princess Royal

Princess Anne, Princess Royal (Anne Elizabeth Alice Louise; born 15 August 1950), is the only daughter of Elizabeth II and Prince Philip, Duke of Edinburgh. At the time of her birth, she was third (behind her mother and elder brother) and rose to second (after her mother's accession) in the line of succession to the thrones of the Commonwealth realms; however, after the birth of two younger brothers and six nieces and nephews she is currently tenth in line.

The seventh holder of the title *Princess Royal*, Anne is known for her charitable work, being the patron of over 200 organisations, and she carries out about 700 royal engagements and public appearances per year. She is also known for equestrian talents; she won two silver and one gold medal at the European Eventing Championships, and is the only member of the British Royal Family to have competed in the Olympic Games. Currently married to Vice-Admiral Sir Timothy Laurence, she has two children from her previous marriage to Mark Phillips and one granddaughter.

Early life and education

Anne was born at Clarence House on 15 August 1950, the second child and only daughter of then Princess Elizabeth, Duchess of Edinburgh, and Philip, Duke of Edinburgh, and second grandchild of King George VI and Queen Elizabeth. Baptised in the Music Room of Buckingham Palace on 21 October 1950, by then Archbishop of York, Cyril Garbett, the Princess's godparents were: the Queen (her maternal grandmother); the Hereditary Princess of Hohenlohe-Langenburg (her paternal aunt); Princess Alice of Greece and Denmark (her paternal grandmother); VAdm the Earl Mountbatten of Burma (her paternal granduncle); and the Hon. and Rev. Andrew Elphinstone (her cousin). By letters patent of Anne's great-grandfather, King George V, the titles of a British prince or princess, and the style *Royal Highness*, were only to be conferred on children and male-line grandchildren of the sovereign, as well as the children of the eldest son of the Prince of Wales. However, on 22 October 1948, George VI issued new letters patent granting these honours to any children of Princess Elizabeth and Prince Philip; otherwise, Anne would merely have been titled by courtesy as Lady Anne Mountbatten. In this way, the children of the heiress presumptive had a Royal and Princely status.

As with royal children before her, a governess, Catherine Peebles, was appointed to look after the Princess and was responsible for her early education at Buckingham Palace; Peebles had also served as governess for Anne's older brother, Charles. When Anne's mother acceded after the death of George VI to the throne as Queen Elizabeth II, Anne was thereafter titled as Her Royal Highness The Princess Anne, but, given her young age at the time, did not attend her mother's coronation.

A Girl Guides company, the 1st Buckingham Palace Company including the Holy Trinity Brompton Brownie pack, was reformed in May 1959, specifically so that, like her mother, Anne could socialise with girls her own age. The Princess Royal was active until 1963, when she went to boarding school. Anne remained under private tutelage until she was enrolled at Benenden School in 1963, leaving five years later with six O-Levels and two A-Levels. Anne's first boyfriend was Andrew Parker Bowles.

On Wednesday, 14 November 1973 (her brother Prince Charles's 25th birthday), Princess Anne married Mark Phillips, then a Lieutenant in the 1st Queen's Dragoon Guards, at Westminster Abbey, in a ceremony that was televised around the world, with an estimated audience of 100 million. Following the wedding, Anne and her husband lived at Gatcombe Park. By 1989, however, the Princess Royal and Mark Phillips announced their intention to separate, as the marriage had been under strain for a number of years. The couple divorced on 23 April 1992.

It was believed that the Queen had offered Phillips an earldom on his wedding day, as was customary for untitled men marrying into the Royal Family. However, Phillips did not accept the offer. The couple had two children, Peter Phillips and Zara Phillips, and so, unusually for the grandchildren of a monarch, they have no title. (However, they are not currently the only children of a British Princess to carry no title: the children of Princess Alexandra, the Queen's cousin, are also untitled.)

On 29 December 2010, The Princess Royal became a grandmother when a baby girl was born to her son Peter Phillips and his wife Autumn. The baby girl, Savannah, is the first grandchild of The Princess Royal.

Kidnapping attempt

As Princess Anne and Mark Phillips were returning to Buckingham Palace on 20 March 1974, from a charity event on Pall Mall, their Princess IV limousine was forced to stop by a Ford Escort. The driver of the Escort, Ian Ball, jumped out and began firing a gun. Inspector James Beaton, the Princess's personal police officer, responded by exiting the limousine in order to shield the Princess and try to disarm Ball. Beaton's firearm, a Walther PPK, jammed, and he was shot by the assailant, as was Anne's chauffeur, Alex Callender, when he tried to disarm Ball. Brian McConnell, a nearby tabloid journalist, also intervened, and was shot in the chest. Ball approached the Royal's car and told Anne of his kidnapping plan, which was to hold the Princess for ransom, the sum given by varying sources as £2 million or £3 million, which he intended to give to the National Health Service. Ball then directed Anne to get out of the car, to which she replied: "Not bloody likely!", and briefly considered hitting Ball. Eventually, she dived out of the other side of the limousine and another passing pedestrian, Ron Russell, punched Ball in the back of the head and then led Anne away from the scene. At that point, Police Constable Michael Hills happened upon the situation; he too was shot by Ball, but not before he called for police backup. Detective Constable Peter Edmonds, who had been nearby, answered and gave chase, finally arresting Ball.

All of the victims were hospitalised, and recovered from their wounds. For his defence of Princess Anne, Beaton was awarded the George Cross, Hills and Russell were awarded the George Medal, and Callender, McConnell and Edmonds were awarded the Queen's Gallantry Medal. Ball pleaded guilty to attempted murder and kidnapping, and was detained under the Mental Health Act.

The incident was the closest in modern times that any individual has come to kidnapping a member of the Royal Family, and prompted higher security levels for the Royals. It also served as the focus of the 2006 Granada Television produced docu-drama, *To Kidnap a Princess*, and inspired story lines in the Tom Clancy novel *Patriot Games* and the Antonia Fraser novel *Your Royal Hostage*.

Second marriage

Anne married Timothy Laurence, then a commander in the Royal Navy, at Crathie Kirk, near Balmoral Castle, on 12 December 1992. The couple chose to marry in Scotland as the Church of England did not allow divorced persons to remarry in its churches, while the Church of Scotland did. In participating in this ceremony, Anne became the first Royal divorcée to remarry since Victoria, Grand Duchess of Hesse and by Rhine, did so in 1905. Like Phillips before him, Laurence received no peerage, and the couple leased a flat in Dolphin Square, London. They later gave up this city home and now reside between an apartment at Buckingham Palace and Gatcombe Park. Anne has no children with Laurence.

Criminal record

The Princess Royal faced court charges in March 2001, when she pleaded guilty to driving at 150 km/h (93 mph) on a dual carriageway, while on her way to Hartpury College in Gloucestershire. She was fined £400 by Cheltenham Magistrate's Court, and had five points added to her driving licence. The following year, she was convicted of a second offence under the Dangerous Dogs Act 1991, after she pleaded guilty to the charge that her dog, Dotty, attacked two boys while she and Laurence were taking the dog for a walk in Windsor Great Park. The Princess was fined £500 by Berkshire Magistrates' Court and ordered to give Dotty more training.

Personal interests

Pharology, the study of lighthouses, is a focus of interest for Princess Anne; she made it an ambition to see personally each of Scotland's 215 lighthouses, often touring them with the Northern Lighthouse Board, of which she is patron. It is thought the interest stems from Anne's visit, when she was five years old, to Tiumpan Head with her mother. Since 1989, Princess Anne also has been patron of Sense, the national charity in the United Kingdom that supports and campaigns for children and adults who are deafblind. It provides specialist information, advice and services to deafblind people, their families, carers and the professionals who work with them. In addition, it supports people who have sensory impairments with additional disabilities. The Princess Royal takes a great interest in the work of this charity and hosts a number of events to raise money for its continued good work in the community and beyond. The Princess Royal is also Royal Patron of young people's charity Catch22, with particular reference to their social enterprise Auto22, a mechanics garage offering apprenticeships to young people in Gravesend, Kent.

The Princess Royal is a Patron of The Blond McIndoe Research Foundation. The Foundation is a registered charity and is the legacy of the famous plastic surgeon Sir Archibald McIndoe who operated on over 600 severely burned airmen during WWII; the men later formed the world renowned Guinea Pig Club. The Blond McIndoe Research Foundation has pioneered leading-edge surgical techniques in skin repair and healing wounds, in particular the treatment of burns. The Princess Royal recently attended its 50th anniversary celebrations held in East Grinstead on 22 March 2011.

Anne has always shown a keen interest in horses and equine pursuits. At the age of 21, the Princess won the individual title at the European Eventing Championship, and was voted the BBC Sports Personality of the Year in 1971. For more than five years she also competed with the British eventing team, winning a silver medal in both individual and team disciplines in the 1975 European Eventing Championship, riding the home-bred Doublet. The following year Anne participated in the 1976 Olympic Games in Montreal as a member of the British team, riding the Queen's horse, Goodwill. Princess Anne assumed the Presidency of the Fédération Équestre Internationale from 1986 until 1994. On 5 February 1987, she became the first Royal to appear as a contestant on a television quiz-show when she competed on the BBC panel game *A Question of Sport*. Her daughter, Zara Phillips is also a keen equestrian competitor. Together with her horse, Toytown, she won individual and team gold medals at the 2005 European Eventing Championship as well as individual gold and team silver medals at the 2006 FEI World Equestrian Games.

Princess Anne was a pupil of the Spanish Riding School in Vienna.

Official duties

The Princess Royal with Vladimir Putin in 2000

The Princess Royal visits the USNS *Comfort* on 11 July 2002, while the ship was docked in Southampton, England.

As Princess Royal, Princess Anne undertakes a number of official duties on behalf of her mother, in her role as sovereign of the Commonwealth realms. Anne receives an annual allowance of £228,000, most of which is spent on staff who support her public engagements and correspondence. Anne began to undertake official royal duties overseas upon leaving secondary school, and accompanied her parents on a state visit to Austria in the same year. She will sometimes stand in for the Queen at the funerals of foreign dignitaries (which the Queen customarily does not attend), and resides at Holyrood Palace in Edinburgh each summer, hosting engagements there. The Princess also travels abroad on behalf of the United Kingdom up to three times a year; she was the first member of the Royal Family to make an official visit to the USSR when she went there as a guest of the government in 1990. The Princess's first tour of Australia was with her parents in 1970, since which she has returned on numerous occasions to undertake official engagements as a colonel-in-chief of an Australian regiment, or to attend memorials and services, such as the National Memorial Service for victims of the Black Saturday bushfires in Melbourne, Australia, on 22 February 2009.

Following the retirement of the Queen Mother in 1981, Anne was elected by graduates of the University of London as that institution's Chancellor. Throughout May 1996, the Princess served as Her Majesty's High Commissioner to the General Assembly of the Church of Scotland, which granted her, for the duration of the appointment, a higher precedence in Scotland, and the alternative style of *Her Grace*. In 2007, the Princess Royal had the honour of being appointed by the Queen as Grand Master of the Royal Victorian Order, a position her late grandmother had also held.

The Princess Royal carries out the most engagements of any member of the Royal Family, and is involved with over 200 charities and organisations in an official capacity. She works extensively for Save the Children, of which she has been president since 1970, and she initiated The Princess Royal Trust for Carers in 1991; her work for the charity takes her all over the world, including many poverty stricken African nations. She is also the Royal Patron of WISE, an organisation that encourages young women to pursue careers in science, engineering and construction. Her extensive work for St. John Ambulance as Commandant-in-Chief of St. John Ambulance Cadets has helped to develop many young people, as she annually attends the Grand Prior Award Reception. She is also a British representative in the International Olympic Committee as an administrator, and is a member of the London Organising Committee for the Olympic Games.

The Princess Royal was elected Chancellor of the University of Edinburgh in 2011, effective 31 March, succeeding her father, Prince Philip, Duke of Edinburgh who stepped down from the role in 2010. She is also Patron of Edinburgh University's Royal (Dick) School of Veterinary Studies, Royal Holloway, University of London, International Students House, London, Acid Survivors Trust International, Townswomen's Guilds and College of Occupational Therapy.

- **15 August 1950 – 6 February 1952**: *Her Royal Highness* Princess Anne of Edinburgh
- **6 February 1952 – 14 November 1973**: *Her Royal Highness* The Princess Anne
- **14 November 1973 – 13 June 1987**: *Her Royal Highness* The Princess Anne, *Mrs* Mark Phillips
- **13 June 1987 – :** *Her Royal Highness* The Princess Royal

The Princess's British style and title in full: *Her Royal Highness The Princess Anne Elizabeth Alice Louise, The Princess Royal, Lady Laurence, Lady of the Most Noble Order of the Garter, Lady of the Most Ancient and Most Noble Order of the Thistle, Dame Grand Cross and Grand Master of the Royal Victorian Order, Dame Grand Cross of the Most Venerable Order of the Hospital of St John of Jerusalem.* In 1996, Anne was entitled to be called Her Grace The Lord High Commissioner to the General Assembly of the Church of Scotland.

Anne is the seventh creation of the title *Princess Royal*, an appellation given only to the eldest daughter of the sovereign, the last holder being George V's daughter, Princess Mary, Countess of Harewood.

Honours
Appointments
- **1969 – :** Royal Family Order of Queen Elizabeth II
- **1971 – 1998**: Dame of Justice of the Most Venerable Order of the Hospital of St John of Jerusalem (DStJ)
  - **1998 – :** Dame Grand Cross of the Most Venerable Order of the Hospital of St John of Jerusalem (GCStJ)
- **1974 – :** Dame Grand Cross of the Royal Victorian Order (GCVO)
- **1986 – :** Fellow of the Royal College of Veterinary Surgeons (FRCVS)
- **1987 – :** Royal Fellow of the Royal Society (FRS)
- **1990 – :** Extra Companion of the Queen's Service Order (QSO)
- **23 April 1994 – :** Royal Lady of the Most Noble Order of the Garter (LG)
- **2000 – :** Lady of the Most Ancient and Most Noble Order of the Thistle (LT)
- **29 September 2005 – :** Chief Grand Companion of the Order of Logohu (GCL)

Decorations
- **2 June 1953**: Queen Elizabeth II Coronation Medal
- **1977**: Queen Elizabeth II Silver Jubilee Medal
- **1982**: Canadian Forces Decoration (CD)
- **2002**: Queen Elizabeth II Golden Jubilee Medal
- **2005**: Commemorative Medal for the Centennial of Saskatchewan

Foreign honours
- **1969**: Grand Decoration of Honour in Gold with Sash for Services to the Republic of Austria
- **1969 – :** Commander Grand Cross of the Order of the White Rose of Finland (SVR SR)
- **1971 – :** Grand Cordon of the Order of the Precious Crown
- **1972 – :** Grand Cross of the Order of the House of Orange
- **1972 – :** Grand Cross of the Order of the Oak Crown
- **1972 – 1991**: Order of the Yugoslav Flag with Sash, 1st Class

Academic
- **2011 – :** University of Edinburgh, Chancellor

Honorary degrees
- **2004**: University of Regina, Doctor of Laws (LLD)
- **23 April 2010**: Memorial University of Newfoundland, Doctor of Laws (LLD)

Honorary military appointments

The Princess Royal on the balcony of Buckingham Palace (in uniform, far right.)

The Princess Royal passes behind the Princess Anne Banner at a parade for the 75th anniversary of the Royal Australian Corps of Signals, 5 July 2000.

As with other senior royals, Princess Anne holds a number of honorary appointments in the armed forces of several Commonwealth realms. In 2002, she became the first non-reigning woman to attend a funeral in uniform when she wore that of the Royal Navy at the funeral of her grandmother, the Queen Mother.

Anne is of the following regiments, corps, and branches:

Australia
- Colonel-in-Chief of the Royal Australian Corps of Signals

Canada
- Colonel-in-Chief of the Grey and Simcoe Foresters
- Colonel-in-Chief of the 8th Canadian Hussars (Princess Louise's)
- Colonel-in-Chief of the Communications and Electronics Branch
- Colonel-in-Chief of the Canadian Forces Medical Service
- Colonel-in-Chief of the Royal Regina Rifles
- Colonel-in-Chief of Royal Newfoundland Regiment

New Zealand
- Colonel-in-Chief of the Royal New Zealand Corps of Signals
- Colonel-in-Chief of the Royal New Zealand Army Nursing Corps

United Kingdom
- Colonel-in-Chief of the King's Royal Hussars
- Colonel-in-Chief of the Worcestershire and Sherwood Foresters Regiment (29/45 Foot)
- Colonel-in-Chief of the Royal Corps of Signals
- Colonel-in-Chief of the Royal Logistic Corps
- Colonel-in-Chief the Royal Army Veterinary Corps
- Colonel of the Blues and Royals
- Royal Colonel of the Royal Scots Borderers, 1st Battalion Royal Regiment of Scotland
- Royal Colonel of the 52nd Lowland Regiment, 6th Battalion Royal Regiment of Scotland
- Royal Honorary Colonel of the University of London OTC
- Commandant-in-Chief of the First Aid Nursing Yeomanry (Princess Royal's Volunteer Corps)
- Honorary Air Commodore of RAF Lyneham
- Honorary Air Commodore of the University of London Air Squadron
- Vice Admiral and Chief Commandant for women of the Royal Navy
- Commodore-in-Chief of HMNB Portsmouth

Source (edited): "http://en.wikipedia.org/wiki/Anne,_Princess_Royal"

Arthur Rook

Arthur Laurence Rook (26 May 1921 – 30 September 1989) was a British equestrian and Olympic champion. He won a team gold medal in *eventing* at the 1956 Summer Olympics in Stockholm. He became European champion in 1953.

Rook was an officer in the British army, the Royal Horse Guards, and served in Egypt and Italy during the Second World War. He received the Military Cross in 1944.

Source (edited): "http://en.wikipedia.org/wiki/Arthur_Rook"

Ben Maher

Ben Maher (born January 30, 1983) is an English equestrian who competes in the sport of show jumping.

Ben is married. His wife is Kathleen Maher, a model and a show jumper as well. Together they live in Great Britain.

2005
CSIO5* Hickstead, Great Britain: Maher won the famous Hickstead Derby with *Alfredo II*

2008
Ben competed at the Olympic Games with *Rolette*.

2010
CSI5*-W s'-Hertogenbosch, The Netherlands: On the 26th March, Maher and *Wonderboy III* took the top spot in the feature class of the opening day. This was the 1.50m Rabobank Prijs worth 8000CHF to the winner.

CSI5*-W London Olympia, Great Britain: Ben and *Noctambule Courcelle* won the Puissance.

2011
CSI5*-W Basel, Switzerland: *Oscar* took 4th prize in a speed-class.

CSI5*-W Zurich, Switzerland: Maher and *Robin Hood W* took second prize of €35,000 in the Rolex FEI World Cup Qualifier.

CSI3* Lummen, Belgium: *Tripple X III* took second prize in the 'Hyundai' Grand Prix of €10,000.

Source (edited): "http://en.wikipedia.org/wiki/Ben_Maher"

Bertie Hill

Albert "Bertie" Edwin Hill (7 February 1927 – 5 August 2005) was a British equestrian.

After serving in the Home Guard during the Second World War, Hill became an amateur jockey in point-to-point racing. He went on to represent Britain in three-day eventing, winning a gold medal at the 1956 games in Stockholm along with a host of other international trophies.

In the 1960s, Hill and his wife opened a riding school at Rapscott on Exmoor, training a number of future international riders including Princess Anne and Captain Mark Phillips.

Source (edited): "http://en.wikipedia.org/wiki/Bertie_Hill"

Brian Turner Tom Lawrence

Brian Turner Tom Lawrence VC (9 November 1873 - 7 June 1949) was an English recipient of the Victoria Cross, the highest and most prestigious award for gallantry in the face of the enemy that can be awarded to British and Commonwealth forces.

Details

Born in Bewdley, Worcestershire, the eldest of five brothers, and the son of Hannah and John Lawrence, a timber merchant of 15, Lower Park, Bewdley. Lawrence was a former pupil of King Charles I Grammar School, Kidderminster.

Lawrence was 26 years old, and a sergeant in the 17th Lancers (Duke of Cambridge's Own), British Army during the Second Boer War when the following deed took place for which he was awarded the VC.

On the 7th August, 1900, when on patrol duty near Essenbosch Farm, Sergeant Lawrence and a Private Hayman were attacked by 12 or 14 Boers. Private Hayman's horse was shot, and the man was thrown, dislocating his shoulder. Sergeant Lawrence at once came to his assistance, extricated him from under the horse, put him on his own horse and sent him on to the picket. Sergeant Lawrence took the soldier's carbine, and wiih his own carbine as well, kept the Boers off until Private Hayman was safely out of range. He then retired for some two miles on foot, followed by the Boers, and keeping them off till assistance arrived.

Further information

He was decorated by King Edward in London in 1902. Lawrence later served in World War I and World War II and reached the rank of lieutenant-colonel in the 18th Royal Hussars (later 13th/18th Royal Hussars).

Olympics

He competed in the 1912 Summer Olympics for Great Britain in eventing. He did not finish the Individual eventing (Military) competition, also the British team did not finish the team event.

The medal

The medal is on display at the Lord Ashcroft VC Gallery in the Imperial War Museum in London.

Source (edited): "http://en.wikipedia.org/wiki/Brian_Turner_Tom_Lawrence"

Bridget Parker (equestrian)

Bridget Parker (born 5 January 1939) is a British equestrian and Olympic champion. She won a team gold medal in eventing at the 1972 Summer Olympics in Munich, and finished tenth in individual eventing. Parker rode a horse named Cornish Gold at the 1972 Olympic Games. The British team gold medal was later called one of the "30 greatest sporting achievements of all time" by Times magazine.

Source (edited): "http://en.wikipedia.org/wiki/Bridget_Parker_(equestrian)"

Caroline Pratt

For the progressive-education pioneer and founder of the City & Country School, see Caroline Pratt (educator).

Caroline Pratt (23 June 1962 – 4 September 2004) was a well-known rider in the equestrian discipline of three-day eventing.

Pratt was born in Lound, Nottinghamshire. She was one of the 14 elite performance riders in the British squad, but was killed in a rotational fall whilst competing at the Burghley Horse Trials near Peterborough, Cambridgeshire, on 4 September 2004, riding her second horse in the competition that day Primitive Streak.

Competitive success

Pratt was placed 7th at the four star Burghley event in 2003 on Primitive Control, and had be long listed for both the Sydney and Athens Olympic squads, although was eventually not selected for either.

Horses after death

On the day of her death, Pratt had already completed the course on first horse Call Again Cavalier, who has gone on to be the Olympic mount of fellow eventer Mary King.

Memorial trust

Following her death, her family set up a memorial trust granting bursaries to aspiring young eventers.

Source (edited): "http://en.wikipedia.org/wiki/Caroline_Pratt"

Christopher Bartle

Christopher Bartle (born 19 February 1952 in Harrogate, North Yorkshire) is a British equestrian who has enjoyed success in both Dressage and Eventing. He is currently the Managing Director of the Yorkshire Riding Centre and from 2001 together with Hans Melzer, he is the German 3 Day Eventing National Team Trainer. Chris is the brother of Jane Bartle-Wilson, who was also an Olympian in the 84' Los Angeles Olympics.

The Early Years

Chris was educated at Ampleforth College and the University of Bristol were he obtained a BSc(Econ) with honours in Economics. After his university years Chris was an amateur jockey, but being 5ft11 he struggled to keep his weight down in order to establish himself. This prompted his first spell in Three day eventing. He was initially trained by his mother, Mrs Nicole Bartle and then later by Hans von Blixen-Finecke, Jr., (A Double Gold Medalist @ the 1952 Helsinki Olympics for Three day Eventing).

Competitor

Dressage

Most notably while preparing for the 76' Burghley Horse Trials his horse picked up a tendon injury that forced the horse into retirement from eventing. But as one door closed another opened, and the same horse showed potential in Dressage. 1 year later he was competing at the World Championships as an individual. That horse was Wily Trout. The combination went on to become part of the British Dressage Team from 1981-1987. In this time he competed at the 84' Summer Olympics in Los Angeles for the British team. The team came 8th, but Chris Bartle tied for 6th in the individual event to make history by becoming the highest placed Brit. A record he still holds to this day (As of January 2011). Chris and Wily Trout's last major contribution in dressage came when they won a Silver medal in the first Nashua Dressage World Cup in S'hertogenbosch, Holland 1986. This period was capped off when he was awarded the British Equestrian Federation's Medal of Honour in 1986.

Three Day Eventing

Bartle then took the opportunity to turn back to eventing and had a whole host of successes which included winning team Gold at the 1997 European Championships with the British Event Team, before winning the prestigious Badminton Horse Trials in 1998, on his horse Word Perfect II. He also travelled with Word Perfect to the Sydney Olympics in 2000, as reserve.

Past Rides

- Dressage - Wily Trout & Honey Tangle
- Eventing - Wily Trout, Up River, Castle Hill, Word Perfect II, Oscar

Trainer

British National Team

After his successful Dressage period Chris was invited to train the British Eventing team, where he went to the 96' Atlanta and 00' Sydney Olympic games. In 1995 Christopher received the British Horse Society's Trainers Award and in 2001 was awarded Honorary Fellowship of the British Horse Society

German National Team

Since 2001 Chris has been the National Coach to the German Olympic Three Day Event Team - Winners of Team and Individual Gold medals at the Beijing Olympics in 2008 and Michael Jung, Individual World Champion Kentucky 2010. His wealth of experience lead to him writing *Training the Sport Horse*, which he co-authored with Gilliam Newsum. The book was published by J. A. Allen in 2004.

Training Individuals

Locally Christopher trains many British International level riders, notably for many years the British team rider Nicola Wilson from Northallerton, North Yorkshire.

Yorkshire Riding Centre

Chris has been the Managing Director and resident instructor at the Yorkshire Riding Centre for many years, developing a wealth of knowledge. He does not exclusively teach international or high level competition riders, and is known to teach developing riders on their own horses.

Accomplishments

Dressage

- Highest placed British Dressage rider in the Olympic Games to date (6th, 1984 Los Angeles Olympics)
- National Dressage Champion in 1984 and 1985
- 4th place at the 1985 European Championships
- 2nd place at the 1986 Nashua Dressage World Cup
- Awarded the British Equestrian Federation's Medal of Honour in 1986.

Eventing

- 1991 Scottish Open Champion (Up River)
- Placed at 1995 Burghley CCI**** (Castle Hill)
- 3rd at 1996 Blenheim ***
- 5th at 1996 Bramham ***
- Completed 1997 Badminton ****
- 1997 Scottish Open Champion

(Word Perfect)
- Team Gold Medal at the 1997 European Championships
- 1st at the 1998 Badminton Horse Trials CCI**** (Word Perfect)
- 1st at the 1999 Achselschwang Horse Trials *** (Oscar)
- 5th at the 2000 Burghley ****

- (Word Perfect)
- Reserve for Sydney 2000 British Event Team (Word Perfect)

Training
- Was awarded the British Horse Society's Trainers Award in 1995
- Dressage Trainer to British Event Team at the 1996 Atlanta and 2000 Sydney Games
- German National Trainer Eventing since 2001 (together with Hans Melzer)
- Was awarded Honorary Fellowship of the British Horse Society in 2001

Source (edited): "http://en.wikipedia.org/wiki/Christopher_Bartle"

Daisy Dick

Daisy Berkeley, formerly known as Daisy Dick (born 29 March 1972 in Oxford) is a British three-day eventing rider. With her horse Spring Along, she won the bronze medal for Great Britain in the team eventing at the 2008 Summer Olympics in Beijing.

In October 2009 she married to Charles Berkeley.

Source (edited): "http://en.wikipedia.org/wiki/Daisy_Dick"

Derek Allhusen

Major **Derek Swithin Allhusen**, CVO (9 January 1914 – 24 April 2000) was an English equestrian who was a 54 year old grandfather when he rode Lochinvar to team gold and individual silver medals at the 1968 Summer Olympics in Mexico.

Derek Swithin Allhusen was born in London and educated at Eton and Trinity College, Cambridge. In 1937 he married The Hon Claudia Betterton. He served throughout the Second World War with 9th Queen's Royal Lancers, being awarded the American Silver Star in 1944.

On returning from Germany he brought back two horses with him and settled in Claxton, Norfolk. He rode one of the horses, Laura when representing Britain in the pentathlon at the 1948 Winter Olympic Games. He eventually took up eventing in 1955, riding Laura's daughter Laurien on two European Championship teams, winning a team gold medal in 1957, then team silver and individual bronze in 1959. In 1961 he bought Irish-bred Lochinvar and rode her in two winning European Championship teams (in 1967 and 1969) as well as the gold and silver at the 1968 Summer Olympics. He was awarded an MBE for his achievements but declined it; feeling his team-mates Richard Meade, Mary Bullen and Reuben Jones also deserved recognition.

On his retirement from the sport he continued as a breeder and Laurien's son Laurieston was ridden to team and individual Olympic gold medals in 1972 Games in Munich, with Richard Meade in the saddle. Allhusen was president of the British Horse Society from 1986 to 1988.

Allhusen was appointed to be one of Her Majesty's Body Guard of the Honourable Corps of Gentlemen at Arms in 1963 , he was appointed Standard Bearer from 1981 to 1984. He was appointed to be a Commander of the Royal Victorian Order in 1983.

In November 1955, 1956 and 1957 he was nominated as a High Sheriff of Norfolk (and appointed in March 1958) in the Queen's Bench Division of the High Court of Justice

Source (edited): "http://en.wikipedia.org/wiki/Derek_Allhusen"

Douglas Stewart (equestrian)

Douglas Norman "Duggie" Stewart (born 24 June 1913 - Doonholm Ayrshire, date of death July 1992 - Midlem Selkirk) - son of Brig General Ian Stewart DSO (Cameronians/Scottish Rifles)and Myra Kennedy of Doonholm Ayrshire (m.1907). Sisters Elizabeth (Hill) and Rhona (m. Colonel Alec Scott of Tetbury). He was a cavalry (equestrian) officer , commanding Royal Scots Greys age 31 in last 6 months of World War 2, and again 1950-1952. He was awarded two Military Crosses and a Distinguished Service Order. He represented Britain at the London Olympics 1948, in the eventing team, and again at the 1952 Helsinki Olympics in the show jumping team, when he won the UK's only Gold Medal with Sir Harry Llewellyn and Wilfe White. He later farmed near Banbury in Oxfordshire - once landing his light aircraft in a field near Aylesbury where the great train robbers were hiding; they cleared out at 2am next morning leaving their finger prints and mail bags empty! - and later in the Scottish Borders near St Boswells. Education - Rugby and Sandhurst. Keen shot, fisherman and dedicated deer stalker. Married Gillian Hollick (from Warwickshire) in 1943; with issue Claire Gillian 1944, Robert Douglas 1945 and Rory 1950 (mother died in childbirth, Rory cot death 10 days later). 2nd wife Phoebe Gosling in 1952 and had issue Ian Norman 1953

and James Patrick 1956.
Source (edited): "http://en.wikipedia.org/wiki/Douglas_Stewart_(equestrian)"

Edward Howard-Vyse

Lieutenant General **Sir Edward Dacre Howard-Vyse** KBE CB MC (27 November 1905 – 26 December 1992) was a British Army General as well as a British horse rider who competed in the 1936 Summer Olympics.

Career

Edward Howard-Vyse was commissioned into the Royal Artillery in 1927.

In 1936 he and his horse *Blue Steel* won the bronze medal as part of the British eventing team, after finishing 19th in the individual eventing competition.

He served in World War II and was promoted to Major in 1942.

After the War he took office as Director Royal Artillery from 1959 to 1961 and then General Officer Commanding-in-Chief of Western Command from 1962 to 1964. He retired in 1964.

He was also Colonel Commandant of the Royal Artillery from 1962 until 1970.

Family

In 1940 he married Mary Bridget Willoughby and together they went on to have two sons and a daughter.

He died in Ryedale in 1992.
Source (edited): "http://en.wikipedia.org/wiki/Edward_Howard-Vyse"

Edward Radcliffe-Nash

Edward Radcliffe-Nash (June 9, 1888 – February 21, 1915) was a British horse rider who competed in the 1912 Summer Olympics.

Education and military Career

Born in London on June 9, 1888 to Lieut-Colonel Edward Nash JP (Late Essex Regiment) of Ballycartee, Tralee, Co. Kerry, and Constance, daughter of John Radcliffe of Moorfield Withington, JP.

Educated at Mr. Bulls Preparatory School, Westgate on Sea (1898 – 1902), Eton (1902 – July 1905) and Sandhurst Military College into which he passed the entrance exams on August 15, 1905 with the position of 119 from a cadetship of 196 receiving 7,838 marks. He commenced his period at Sandhurst Military College in September 1905. Edward Radcliffe Nash left Eton at the earliest possible moment (giving up all that Eton could give him over the next two years) to enroll at Sandhurst to enable him to gain seniority in the Army. In July 1906 Edward Radcliffe Nash graduated from Sandhurst Military College with the position of 87 from 218 cadets. On August 29, 1906, Edward Radcliffe Nash was gazetted as 2nd Lieutenant into the 16th Lancers and joined his Regiment on October 3, 1906. He was promoted to Lieutenant on January 15, 1909 and Captain on October 10, 1914. Edward Radcliffe Nash qualified at the School of Musketry in their examinations on October 14, 1910.

He went to France with the British Expeditionary Force (BEF) in August 1914. He took part in the retreat from Mons, the battles of the Marne, the Aisne and the First Battle of Ypres. He was killed in action near Ypres on February 21, 1915, when the 16th Lancers suffered severely through the blowing up of a trench. At the time of his death he was acting Adjutant of his Regiment. Captain Edward Radcliffe Nash was mentioned in Lord John French's Dispatches of 8 October 1914 (London Gazette October 19, 1914).

Sporting career

Edward Radcliffe Nash was a splendid all round sportsman. He distinguished himself at Eton as a long distance runner and as a "wet bob". In 1905 he won the Junior Sculls and stroked his Junior House Four up to "head", the last time that the colours of Miss Evan's were seen on the river.

Whilst at Sandhurst he proved himself to be a remarkable athlete, winning against competitors considerably older than himself in the equivalent of the "Victor Ludorum" cup. After joining the 16th Lancers he ran twice in the Army Championship for the mile, being second on both occasions with practically no training. However he devoted himself to riding. He was well known at Olympia and represented Britain at the Stockholm Olympic Games in 1912. He did not finish the Individual eventing (Military) competition, also the British team did not finish the team event. However in the individual jumping event he finished 29th on *The Flea*.

He was first and second in successive years at the Grafton Pont-to-Point, won his Regimental Light Weight Steeplechase on two occasions and was "placed" at a number of other meetings at which he rode.

In De Ruvigny's Roll Of Honour 1914 – 1924 it is said that : - "As conspicuous for dash, energy and endurance in War as in sport, he was the ideal cavalry officer and appeared to have a distinguished career before him. His exuberant vitality found expression in all that he said or did, and one who knew him well, observed on hearing that he had been killed: "Of all the deaths in this war, his death is the hardest to realise"."

Captain Edward Radcliffe Nash is buried in the Ypres Town Cemetery, Ieper, West-Vlaanderen, Belgium, Row G, Grave 4.

Captain Edward Radcliffe Nash had a younger brother, Llewellyn Charles Nash (a Captain in the King's Royal Rifle Corps) who died of wounds on

September 28, 1915.

Source (edited): "http://en.wikipedia.org/wiki/Edward_Radcliffe-Nash"

Ellen Whitaker

Ellen Whitaker (born March 5, 1986) is a British female show jumping rider, ranked 7th by the British Showjumping Association for May 2005 to April 2006. She is the daughter of rider Steven Whitaker and niece of riders John Whitaker and Michael Whitaker. She lives in Barnsley, South Yorkshire.

Whitaker's achievements include:
- Winner of the 2009 Horse of the Year show Show Jumper of the year Grand Prix, and Show Jumper of the show.
- Three times winner of the Horse of the Year Show Speed stakes (2006, 2008+2009)
- Winner of the Horse of the Year Show 2009 Puissance
- Area UK Special GP 2009
- BSJA Leading Under-21 Rider and Members Personality of the Year 2005
- Winner of the Longines Ladies Award for Elegance in Barcelona
- Winner of the 2007 Hickstead Speed Derby
- Winner of the Young Riders Championship at the Horse of the Year Show 2005
- Member of the European Bronze Medal Winning Team 2007 and Silver Medal 2003
- and a variety of other prizes and awards

British Ranking: 6th (Leading Lady)
World Ranking: Dec 2007 = 60th

Ellen Whitaker has 12 horses, one of which is AK Locarno, also known as Locarno 62, whose purchase price of EUR 1,000,000 in 2005 made him the most expensive horse ever imported to the UK. Locarno is a bay Holsteiner stallion, owned by Mrs D. Makin and Mr S. Whitaker. Since 2008, Locarno 62 has been Whitaker's top horse. Locarno 62's leg infection in June 2008 caused Whitaker to miss qualifying for the 2008 Summer Olympics.

She is also known for riding the horses Magic Max (who was reputedly sold for £1,000,000 in 2003) and Naff Naff II, on whom she came in third nationally at the Southview Jumping Show in the 1.40m class in 2006.

Her more recent horses include Ladina B (Puissance and 6 Bar Specialist), CS Online, Equimax Ocolado (who partnered her to HOYS Leading show jumper of the year victory), Sherwater Mikado, Sefana, Kansilier, Henri de Here and numerous youngsters to be brought on.

She just missed out on selection for the Beijing Olympics '08, due to a lameness in AK Locarno 62. Locarno was due to return to jumping in late 2009.

On May 4 2011, it was reported in multiple sources that Whitaker was engaged to actor Henry Cavill.

Source (edited): "http://en.wikipedia.org/wiki/Ellen_Whitaker"

Elwyn Hartley Edwards

Elwyn Hartley Edwards, MC, equestrian writer and editor, was born on 17 April 1927. He died on 9 December 2007, aged 80.

Elwyn Edwards, was the editor of Riding magazine for 18 years. And the consultant editor for *Horse & Hound magazine* for five years, he also served as a regional chairman of the British Horse Society and as a member of the BHS council, receiving the society's Award of Merit in 1993. He was also a vice-president of the Riding for the Disabled Association and vice-patron of the Horse and Pony Protection Association.

He used to regularly judge horse shows in the UK. He had written more than 30 books on horse-related subjects and was an authority on lorinery and saddlery.

Source (edited): "http://en.wikipedia.org/wiki/Elwyn_Hartley_Edwards"

Emma Hindle

Emma Hindle (born 19 May 1975) is a British international equestrian. She first rode for her country in 2004, competing in the World Equestrian Games of that year, and competed for Great Britain in Dressage at both the Athens and Beijing Olympic Games.

Early life
Hindle was born in Preston, Lancashire on 19 May 1975. After riding a donkey on the beach at Blackpool aged 4, she began taking regular riding lessons at her aunts stables. She began competitive showing in Working hunter classes, followed by eventing.

Career
Aged 12, Hindle was under instruction from international dressage judge Stephen Clarke and at 18 she moved to Sweden to train with Kyra Kyrklund at the Flyinge Stud.

When Kyrklund moved to the UK in 1993, Hindle moved to the base of Netherlands Olympic dressage medallist Ellen Bontje in Frankfurt, Germany. It was from this base that she competed in the Beijing Olympics.

Now running the Brookhouse Stud in Erbach, Rhineland-Palatinate, Hindle is part of the London 2012 World Class Performance Programme.

Source (edited): "http://en.wikipedia. org/wiki/Emma_Hindle"

Flora Harris

Flora Harris (born 21 March 1988 in London, later moving to live near Taunton, before setting up her own yard near Banbury in Oxfordshire, is an eventrider who became a full senior in 2010. In 2007, she competed for Great Britain at the Young Rider European Eventing Championships at Blair Castle, Scotland. She has been shortlisted twice for the junior team, in 2005 and 2006, and in 2007, her first year as young rider (18–21 years) was selected as an individual on the young rider squad. In 2008, Harris won the CIC 2* at Osberton. In 2008 she was selected for the long list for the Young Rider European Squad. She was long-listed for Young Rider squad in 2008 and 2009, but prevented from squad selection in 2008 by horse injury and in 2009 by breaking her leg. Flora was runner-up with Law Choice and placed on Double Image 11 at Vale Sabroso in February 2009 and placed on Law Choice and Boy at Barroca de Alva in March 2009. In 2010, she took Boy and Law Choice to Barroca de Alva for 2* and 3* competition in which Boy was 13th and Law Choice 5th.

In 2008, Harris was a columnist for *Eventing Worldwide*. In 2009, Harris became a columnist for www.horsehero.com and submits a regular blog.

In 2009 she had a shorter season as she broke her leg. Flora invited onto BEF Regional Foundation Squad, South West region.

In 2010 was runner-up under 25 national Championship on Law Choice and winner of Express Eventing at the Festival of the Horse in July. Law Choice has remained listed in the top 20 performing horses in the UK for the whole season.

In 2011 Flora had her fist attempt at Badminton 4* with Law Choice. After dressage and cross country she was in the top 20 before a slight injury to Law Choice cause wiwthdrawal. Flor'a performance attracted very positive feedback.

At the end of 2010, Flora was ranked 26th in UK and 129 out of 3300 worldwide. Flora a

At the moment Harris rides 8 horses: Law Choice, Candice by Canabis Z, Boy by Kashmir von Schuttershof, Amazing Mazy by Adelante, It's Without Prejudice by It's Without Doubt, Canadian Sky, Faerie Concorde for the Downey family, It's the Law.

She also has young horses for training

Brendonhill Bon Chance, Highley Prized, Brendonhill Final Role, Just Imagine.

Source (edited): "http://en.wikipedia. org/wiki/Flora_Harris"

Francis Weldon

Francis William Weldon MVO MBE MC (2 August 1913 – 21 September 1993) was a British equestrian and Olympic champion. He won a team gold medal in *eventing* at the 1956 Summer Olympics in Stockholm, and received an individual bronze medal. He became European champion in 1953, 1954 and 1955.

Weldon was a Lieutenant Colonel in the British Army and was Officer Commanding, the King's Troop, Royal Horse Artillery.

Source (edited): "http://en.wikipedia. org/wiki/Francis_Weldon"

Geoff Billington

Geoff Billington is a British showjumper who has represented Great Britain on a number of occasions including during the European and World Championships and at the Olympics. As of Jan 2010, Geoff was ranked 13th on the Team GBR list.

Early life

Geoff Billington was born on 2nd March 1955, and started riding at the age of nine year old at a local riding school. He went to serve an apprenticeship with showjumper David Bowen.

Career achievements

Geoff Billington has competed once in 1998 at the World Championships, achieving a team bronze medal, and also has a European championship team bronze medal from 1997, although he also competed there in 1999 and 2009.

He has represented the UK at the Olympics in both 1996 in Atlanta and 2000 in Sydney and has competed in 46 Nations Cups since 1976, with a total of 9 wins.

Billington has also won the British Jumping Derby at Hickstead in 2007, on grey horse Cassabachus, narrowly missing out on the same title a year later to William Funnell.

Source (edited): "http://en.wikipedia. org/wiki/Geoff_Billington"

Harry Llewellyn

Sir Harry Morton Llewellyn, 3rd Baronet, CBE (18 July 1911 – 15 November 1999) was a British equestrian champion. He was born in Aberdare, South Wales, the son of a colliery owner, Sir David Llewellyn, 1st Baronet.

Background

A younger son, he only inherited the baronetcy on the death of his brother in 1978. His younger brother Sir David Llewellyn was a Conservative politician.

Cambridge University & the Army

Llewellyn was educated at Oundle School and at Trinity College, Cambridge, before going into the army.

Early career

He achieved some success as a show-jumping champion during the 1930s, and competed in the Grand National steeplechase, coming second in 1936.

World War II

During World War II he saw action in Italy and after D Day in Normandy and served as a liaison officer to Field Marshal Montgomery, eventually rising to the rank of Colonel in the British Army.

Olympic Gold Medal, Fame & Foxhunter

In 1952 he secured a gold medal in show jumping, at the Helsinki Olympic Games for the British equestrian team, riding the legendary "Foxhunter". Foxhunter died in 1959. After Sir Harry's death, his own ashes were scattered near Foxhunter's grave on the Blorenge mountain above Abergavenny.

Family & Personal Life

Sir Harry Llewellyn lived near Abergavenny in Monmouthshire. In 1990 he was inducted into the Welsh Sports Hall of Fame.

He was married to Christine Saumarez, a daughter of the 5th Baron de Saumarez.

Their sons, Dai and Roddy, became well-known media personalities from the 1960s onwards, the former because of highly publicized relationships with Tessa Dahl and Orson Welles's daughter Beatrice, and the latter because of an eight-year affair with Princess Margaret, Countess of Snowdon.

Source (edited): "http://en.wikipedia.org/wiki/Harry_Llewellyn"

Harvey Smith (equestrian)

Harvey Smith (born 29 December 1938) is a former British show jumping champion.

Smith was born in the West Riding of Yorkshire, and still maintains his stables at Craiglands Farm, High Eldwick, Bingley, near Bradford. He stood out from the ranks of showjumpers because of his broad accent and blunt manner. His career was often controversial; in 1971 he was disciplined (overturned on appeal) after he gave a "V sign" to the judges following a near perfect round which won him the British Show Jumping Derby for the second year in succession. Smith became so famous that he embarked on a brief, but unsuccessful, singing career. His son, Robert, also became an equestrian champion.

Competing in two Summer Olympics, Smith's best finish was fourth in the individual show jumping event at Munich in 1972. He later became a television commentator for the British Broadcasting Corporation, doing equestrian coverage at the 1984 Summer Olympics in Los Angeles.

In 1989 Smith was honoured for being the first man to have jumped in 100 Volvo World Cup Qualifying Rounds.

During the 1970s in his spare time he competed in professional wrestling. In 1975 Smith also made a record titled "True Love".

Source (edited): "http://en.wikipedia.org/wiki/Harvey_Smith_(equestrian)"

Helen Preece

Helen Preece circa 1913

Helen Preece (1897-?) was a British Olympic equestrian who also rode in America.

Biography

She was the daughter of Ambrose Preese, of Fulham road, London.
Source (edited): "http://en.wikipedia.org/wiki/Helen_Preece"

Herbert Scott (equestrian)

Herbert Stuart Lauriston Scott (born December 29, 1885 - died ?) was a British horse rider who competed in the 1912 Summer Olympics.

He did not finish the Individual eventing (Military) competition, also the British team did not finish the team event.

In the individual jumping event he finished fourth.

Source (edited): "http://en.wikipedia.org/wiki/Herbert_Scott_(equestrian)"

Jane Gregory

Jane Gregory (née **Jane Bredin** 30 June 1959 – 1 April 2011), was an international equestrian. She first rode for her country in 1994, competing in the World Equestrian Games of that year, and competed for Great Britain in Dressage at the Atlanta and Beijing Olympic Games.

Early life

Born in Bromley, Kent, Gregory came from a non-equestrian family. At the age of seven she started to learn to ride, going weekly to a riding centre near her home in Cornwall. Her first horse was called Timolin, a Connemara, and was bought for her by her godmother for £175. She joined the North Cornwall Pony Club, winning the junior section of club's championships in 1976.

International career

Her international career started in 1994. In that year she competed in the World Equestrian Games. She rode at the Atlanta Olympics 1996 with her horse Cupido. For several years after this she did not compete internationally due to horse injuries, but by 2001 she was first in the small tour rankings. She made a full comeback in 2006 when she won grand prix and grand prix special with he horse Lucky Star at Munich CDI in May, then she won the grand prix freestyle at the Mariakalnok CDI.

Her last coach was Ulla Salzgeber. She competed in Dressage for Team GB at the Beijing Olympics, stating "I am in a state of shock" upon finding out that she was selected. She was a member of the GB dressage team along with Laura Bechtolsheimer and Emma Hindle.

Personal life

Based from Great Cheverell, Wiltshire, in 2006 Jane married her partner of twenty years, Hong Kong dressage rider Aram Gregory. Gregory died on 1 April 2011 after suffering a heart attack at the age of 51.
Source (edited): "http://en.wikipedia.org/wiki/Jane_Gregory"

Jane Holderness-Roddam

Jane Holderness-Roddam (née Bullen) was born on the 1st July 1948 and is a British event rider, winning Badminton Horse Trials in 1968 (on 'Our Nobby') and 1978 (on 'Warrior'). She also won Burghley Horse Trials in 1976 (on 'Warrior'), and competed in the 1968 Summer Olympics in Mexico City, winning team gold for Great Britain, alongside Richard Meade, Reuben Jones, Mary Bullen-Jane.

Currently Mrs Holderness-Roddam owns a stables in Gloucestershire jointly with her husband.
Source (edited): "http://en.wikipedia.org/wiki/Jane_Holderness-Roddam"

Jeanette Brakewell

Jeanette Brakewell, born 4 February 1974, has been riding since the age of four and is a competitive professional Event Rider.

She was a member of both the British silver medal team at the Athens Olympics of 2004, and the silver medal team in the same event at the Summer Olympics in Sydney 2000 riding her top horse, Over to You.

With Over to You Brakewell was for several years a regular member of the British three day eventing team. Arguably her best achievement to date was in winning the individual silver medal on this horse at the 2002 FEI World Equestrian Games in Jerez, Spain, 2002 and a team bronze medal at the same event. With this horse she was a team gold medallist on four occasions at the European Eventing Championships (1999, 2001, 2003, 2005). Over to You was retired from four star level eventing in 2007. He still competes in lower levels following his career in which, besides competing at the Olympics, he completed Badminton Horse Trials a record seven times.
Source (edited): "http://en.wikipedia.org/wiki/Jeanette_Brakewell"

Joanne Eccles

Joanne Eccles (born 16 February 1989) is a British equestrian who competes in the discipline of vaulting. She won the gold medals in the women's individual events at both the 2009 European Championship and the 2010 FEI World Equestrian Games. Her sister Hannah also represents Great Britain in vaulting.
Source (edited): "http://en.wikipedia.org/wiki/Joanne_Eccles"

John Saint Ryan

John Saint Ryan (born 1953) is a British actor, horse trainer, and equestrian. Ryan has appeared in supporting roles in film and television. His more memorable characters include Fergus in the 1997 Fox television series *Roar* and Myles Standish in the 1994 Disney film *Squanto: A Warrior's Tale*.

Ryan made his acting debut in 1983 in *G.B.H.* and soon landed a small role in the hit British soap opera *Emmerdale* (then known as *Emmerdale Farm*) as Jameson. Ryan appeared in theatre productions of *Far from the Madding Crowd* and *A Streetcar Named Desire*, and in supporting roles in films and television series including *Coronation Street*, *Buffy the Vampire Slayer*, *General Hospital*, *Murder, She Wrote*, *Cybill*, and the made-for-TV movie *The Heidi Chronicles*. Ryan also played the main antagonist Cyborg in *American Cyborg: Steel Warrior*.

Ryan moved to California in the early 1990s. He owns and operates the Red Rose Ranch, a working horse and cattle ranch near Inyokern, California, where he raises, boards, and sells horses. He trains horses and riders in both dressage and western riding; Ryan's specialty is the *doma vaquera* style of western riding, a Spanish form of competitive Western pleasure riding. He has won multiple national and international titles in the sport, and he has written books and produced videos on the *doma vaquera* style.
Source (edited): "http://en.wikipedia.org/wiki/John_Saint_Ryan"

John Whitaker (equestrian)

John Whitaker MBE (born August 5, 1955)(has been riding since the age of six) is a British equestrian and former Olympian. Horses he has partnered include Ryan's Son, Milton and Gammon in the sport of show jumping. Milton is arguably the horse Whitaker is the most famous for riding; having competed him successfully several times at olympic levels.

He has three children — Joanne, Louise and Robert. Robert Whitaker has successfully show jumped at the highest levels. John's niece Ellen Whitaker, nephew William Whitaker and younger brother Michael Whitaker are also show jumpers.

John's wife Clare helps run the yard, arranging show entries and administration. They run a business called John Whitaker International which sells horse equipment.

Source (edited): "http://en.wikipedia.org/wiki/John_Whitaker_(equestrian)"

Kristina Cook

Kristina Cook also known as **Tina Cook** (born August 31, 1970, Rustington), is a British three-day eventing rider. She is the daughter of the four times British jump racing Champion Jockey, Josh Gifford.

With her horse Miner's Frolic she won bronze medals in both the individual and team eventing at the 2008 Summer Olympics in Beijing. Cook only made the Olympic Eventing team, after the withdrawals of granddaughter of Queen Elizabeth II, Zara Phillips and Lucy Wiegersma. She became double European Eventing champion in 2009 on Miner's Frolic in both the Individual and Team competitions at the chamipionships at Fontainebleau in France.

Her achievements prior to the 2008 Olympics included winning gold medals at the 1994 World Equestrian Games in The Hague and the 1995 and 1999 European Championships.

Source (edited): "http://en.wikipedia.org/wiki/Kristina_Cook"

Laura Bechtolsheimer

Laura Bechtolsheimer (b 31 January 1985, Mainz, Germany) is a British dressage rider competing at Olympic level. As of 30 April 2011 the Fédération Equestre Internationale (FEI) rank her 3rd in the world riding Mistral Hojris and 23rd on Andretti H.

A granddaughter of the billionaire property magnate Karl-Heinz Kipp who founded the Massa chain of department stores, she was born in Mainz, Germany in 1985 to parents Wilfried, an entrepreneur and horse trainer, and Ursula. She has three brothers, Felix, a singer with rock group Hey Negrita who battled heroin addiction and now tours prisons helping others, Goetz, and Till.

The family moved to Ampney St Peter in Gloucestershire when she was one and she started riding aged three having been given a pony called Peacock for her birthday. She went on to compete in Pony Club eventing and won the National Championships of Independent Schools at Stonar School aged 12. Bechtolsheimer started to concentrate on dressage aged 13 and was selected to ride at the Pony European Championship the following season, winning a team silver medal at her first major competition. In 2005 she became the youngest British dressage champion at age 20, riding Douglas Dorsey. She graduated from Bristol University in 2007 with a BSc in Philosophy and Politics. She competed in the 2008 Olympic Games on Mistral Hojris, gaining 18th place in the Individual Grand Prix Special and 6th place in the team event and was named as British Dressage's Rider of the Year. At the 2010 FEI World Equestrian Games held in Kentucky USA Bechtolsheimer surpassed her personal best scores and gained three British International Grand Prix records with Mistral Hojris getting 82.511% in the Grand Prix, 81.708% in cial and 85.350% in the Grand Prix Freestyle, gaining her three silver medals, being beaten only by the celebrated Edward Gal and Moorlands Totilas.

Outside of her dressage activities, she is a presenter for equine video website HorseHero.com and is considering a career in public relations and marketing.

Source (edited): "http://en.wikipedia.org/wiki/Laura_Bechtolsheimer"

Leslie Law

Leslie Law (born 5 May 1965, Hereford) is a British eventer, who won the individual gold medal in the 2004 Summer Olympic Games. He started riding at age 10, competing with his brother, and participated in his first accredited event in 1982. He attended Lady Hawkins' School, where his passion for riding really shone. By 1989, he was a widely respected competitor, and that year placed 8th at the Badminton Horse Trials. After a period of consolidation, by the late 1990s he was counted amongst the sport's elite, placing in the top ten at Badminton, Burghley and the British Championship on a number of occasions.

In 1997 he began to compete on the brothers Shear H2O and Shear L'eau, a pair of Irish Sport Horse greys that made him immediately recognisable on the cross-country course. On the former, he won at Bramham in 1999, came second and third at Badminton in 2000 and 2002, and was a member of the British team that won silver at the 2000 Olympic Games and bronze at the 2002 World Equestrian Games. On Shear L'eau, he won team gold at the European Championship.

Their greatest success, however, was at the 2004 Olympics. Tenth after the dressage section, an excellent cross country still left him out of the medals, an inspired clear round in the show jumping saw him awarded the silver medal. However, amid much controversy the result was appealed, as video evidence showed that the gold medalist, German rider Bettina Hoy, had crossed the start line twice, and thus incurred twelve penalty points. By the time the Court of Arbitration for Sport ruled against Hoy, promoting Law to the gold, he had returned to England and heard the news that he was Olympic Champion while competing in the Solihull Horse Trials.

Source (edited): "http://en.wikipedia.org/wiki/Leslie_Law"

Lizzie Purbrick

Elizabeth Mary Josephine Purbrick (née Boone, born 16 May 1955 at Warren Farm, West Acre, Norfolk) is a winner of an Armada Dish at the Badminton Horse Trials in 1984 having competed several times with several mounts including Peter the Great and in many different events. In 1978 she went as an individual to the World Championships at Lexington, Kentucky and came a creditable 16th. There were no less than 22 retirements on the cross country phase. She was part of the British team selected for the 1980 Olympics which the British team attended in part, the British government taking no official position on the US-led boycott. In 1981 she was a member of the team that won a European Gold Medal at Horsens, Denmark. Purbrick retired after being ousted by the equine institution after she moved to South Africa. She now coaches young people in horsemanship and runs a small farm breeding horses and maintaining a parrot sanctuary.

Source (edited): "http://en.wikipedia.org/wiki/Lizzie_Purbrick"

Louise Skelton

Louise Skelton on Bit Of A Barney at Badminton Horse Trials 2010

Louise Skelton is a British equestrian athlete competing in eventing at top three and four star events, and has won at the CCI *** Blair Castle event. She primarily competes on two full brothers, bred by herself, Bit of a Barney and Partly Pickled, although also rides other horses in events of different stature.

Biography

Louise has been a professional rider since 2007, although was competing as a high level amateur prior to that, whilst working part time in Marketing following degree studies at Cardiff University.

She is based in Eardisley in Herefordshire.

Source (edited): "http://en.wikipedia.org/wiki/Louise_Skelton"

Lucinda Green

Lucinda Green MBE (born 7 November 1953, Andover, Hampshire, England) is a champion British equestrian and journalist who was born as **Lucinda Jane Prior-Palmer**.

Family

Lucinda's parents were the late Major-General George Erroll Prior-Palmer (died 1977) and Lady Doreen Hersey Winifred Hope, a daughter of the second Marquess of Linlithgow, who served as Viceroy of India from 1936 to 1943. Her other grandfather was Prior Spunner Prior-Palmer, of Dublin, and she has an older brother called Simon Erroll Prior-Palmer.

Early life
She went to the independent St Mary's School in Wantage.

Personal life
Lucinda married the Australian equestrian David Green in 1981 in Salisbury and they have a son Fred (born May 1985) and daughter Lissa (born February 1989), but divorced in 1992.

Career
She began riding at age four, and is most known for winning the Badminton Horse Trials a record six times, on six different horses: Be Fair (1973), Wideawake (1976), George (1977), Killaire (1979), Regal Realm (1983), and Beagle Bay (1984).

To date, Green is the only rider to have done so. She has also won the Tony Collins Trophy—given to the British rider with the most points in eventing in a season, a record seven times.

Green first represented Britain at the 1973 European Championships at Kiev. She competed in the European Championships a total of 7 times, and was European Champion in both 1975, on Be Fair, and in 1977, on George.

She attended her first Olympics in 1976, at the Montreal Games. However, she had to retire after cross-country after her mount, Be Fair, slipped a tendon on course. She returned to represent Britain in 1980, at the alternative Olympics at Fontainbleau, where she was rose from 69th place after dressage to 7th place, following a stellar cross-country ride.

Green's 1981 career included a win at the world-renowned Burghley Horse Trials.

In 1982, she went on to represent the British Team at the World Championships in Luhmuhlen, where the team won gold. She also was part of the silver medal British Team at the 1983 European Championships in Switzerland, where she also won an individual silver medal.

In 1984, Green attended Badminton, and not only won for the sixth time, on Beagle Bay, but also placed fifth. Later that year, at the Los Angeles Olympics, she represented the silver medal British Team and individually placed 6th.

Green became a mother in 1985, and she retired for a few months before returning to international competition later that year and helping the British Team win the gold at the European Championships held at Burghley. She was short-listed to attend the 1986 World Championships as well, but an injury to her horse forced her to withdraw. However, in late 1986 she went on to win the event at Boekelo.

Green finished her international career after attending the 1987 European Championships in Luhmuhlen. She now is a commentator for major events, and conducts clinics worldwide. Green is also a member of the Board of Directors of the British Horse Trials Association and a team selector

Red Mile Entertainment released the video game "Lucinda Green's Equestrian Challenge" for the PlayStation 2 game console on 16 November 2006

Major accomplishments
- Six-time Badminton winner
- Seven-time Tony Collins Memorial Trophy winner

1987
- Member of British Team at World Championships at Luhmuhlen

1986
- 1st at Boekelo

1985
- Team gold medal at the European Championships at Burghley

1984
- Team silver at Los Angeles Olympic Games
- 6th Individually at Los Angeles Olympic Games
- 1st Badminton Horse Trials (Beagle Bay)

1983
- 1st Badminton Horse Trials (Regal Realm)
- Team silver at European Championships in Switzerland
- Individual silver at European Championships in Switzerland

1982
- World Champion of Eventing
- Team gold at World Championships at Luhmuhlen

1981
- 1st place Burghley Horse Trials (Beagle Bay)

1980
- 7th place individually at Alternative Olympics in Fontainbleau
- 1st Melbourne—Novice and Open Classes on borrowed horses

1979
- 1st Badminton Horse Trials (Killaire)

1977
- 1st Badminton Horse Trials (George)
- 1st European Championship (George)
- 1st Burghley Horse Trials (George)

1976
- 1st Badminton Horse Trials (Wideawake)
- Member of British Team at Montreal Olympics (Be Fair)

1975
- 1st European Championship (Be Fair)

1973
- 1st Badminton Horse Trials (Be Fair)
- Member of British Team at Kiev

info from reference.com
Source (edited): "http://en.wikipedia.org/wiki/Lucinda_Green"

Madeleine Gurdon

Madeleine Astrid Gurdon, Baroness Lloyd-Webber, (born 30 November 1962) is an English former equestrian sportswoman, and the third and current wife of musical theatre impresario Andrew Lloyd Webber.

Since she is the wife of a peer, and not a peer in her own right, she is referred to as Lady Lloyd-Webber. This is a courtesy title, and she would only be entitled to style herself as Baroness Lloyd-Webber if, for instance, she was created a life peer. This, however, is not the case.

Early life
Born in 1962, She is the daughter of a British Army Brigadier, She was a former equestrian competitor who started a country wear clothing company to supplement her riding career, it was called The Done Thing after her favorite dun horse, Gurdon met Lloyd Webber through his Watership Down neighbours, who loved horses.

Personal life
Gurdon married Lloyd Webber at his Hampshire home on 9 February 1991. They have 3 children together Alastair (born 1992), William (born 1993) and Isabella (born 1996). The family currently reside in South London and Watership Down, Hampshire.
Source (edited): "http://en.wikipedia.org/wiki/Madeleine_Gurdon"

Marion Rose Halpenny

Marion Rose Halpenny is an equestrian writer and horsewoman, born in Lincoln, Lincolnshire, and known as the *Lincolnshire turf authoress*, who has written a number of articles and books on racing, but is mainly known for her pioneering book *British Racing and Racecourses*, which was the first book of its kind and raised interest due to the author being a woman, which was still in 1960s/70s a male dominated area. The book is a detailed list of all the racecourses in the British Isles along with illustrations and guides to each racecourse and its track surface. This exhaustive work had not been done before.

In preparing the information for *British Racing and Racecourses*, she visited 60 of the 62 courses dealt with in the book, (the odd ones were Ayr and Perth) and used a lot of the information she gleaned as a horsewoman and racehorse owner. She knew from personal experience that horses with low numbers in the draw are at a considerable disadvantage at Edinburgh. One of the highlights while she was an owner came on this course when her horse *Calm Palm*, was drawn on the inside and although he was badly bumped by the other horses on the courses slight elbow, he valiantly came from behind to finish second.

She was in the mid 1980's still involved with Racehorses and a project helping ordinary people to become involved in the sport of Kings.

She is married to the British military historian Bruce Barrymore Halpenny. They have a son, commercial artist and writer, Baron Barrymore Halpenny.
Source (edited): "http://en.wikipedia.org/wiki/Marion_Rose_Halpenny"

Mark Armstrong (equestrian)

Mark Armstrong (born 23 June 1964) is a British international show jumper.

Armstrong gained a silver medal at the 1993 European Championships, and came second in the H&H Foxhunter category in the following year's British Horse of the Year Show. He competed in the 2002 World Championships in Leipzig and has been a member of the British team at 33 different events since 1987. He was a member of the four-person British team which finished third at the 2010 FEI Nations Cup of France, riding *Thesaura*.
Source (edited): "http://en.wikipedia.org/wiki/Mark_Armstrong_(equestrian)"

Mark Phillips

Mark Anthony Peter Phillips, CVO, ADC(P) (born 22 September 1948) is a British Olympic gold-medal-winning horseman and ex-husband of Anne, Princess Royal. He is the son of Major Peter William Garside Phillips (1920–1998) and Anne Patricia Phillips (née Tiarks) (1926–1988).
Mark Phillips was educated at Stouts Hill Preparatory School and Marlborough College, whence he joined the Royal Military Academy Sandhurst.

Army
Upon passing out from Sandhurst, Phillips was commissioned as a second lieutenant into the Queen's Dragoon Guards in July 1969. After the expected period, he was promoted to lieutenant in January 1971. By the start of 1974, Phillips was an acting captain when he was appointed a Personal Aide-de-Camp to Queen Elizabeth II. Phillips was substantively promoted to captain in July 1975. Phillips retired from the Army on 30 March 1978.

After retiring from the Army, Phillips continued to style himself Captain Mark Phillips. Ordinarily, only Army officers of or above the rank of major may use their rank when retired. However, retired junior cavalry officers whose civilian work involves equestrianism may continue to use their rank.
In 1972, Phillips was a member of the British three-day event team, which won the gold medal at the Munich Olympics. He won the Badminton Horse Trials in 1971 and 1972 riding *Great Ovation*, in 1974 on *Colombus*, and in 1981 on Lincoln.

In 1998, Phillips designed the cross-country venue for the Red Hills Horse Trials, a qualifying event for the Olympics located in Tallahassee, Florida, USA.

It was through his equestrian activities that he met Princess Anne, only daughter of Queen Elizabeth II and Prince Philip, Duke of Edinburgh.

He is now a regular columnist in *Horse & Hound* magazine. He also remains a leading figure in British equestrian circles and serves as *Chef d'Equipe* of the United States Eventing Team.

First marriage

Phillips married Princess Anne on 14 November 1973, at Westminster Abbey, and had two children:
- Peter Mark Andrew Phillips, born 1977
- Zara Anne Elizabeth Phillips, born 1981

The Queen is believed to have offered him a peerage on his wedding day, which he turned down. This may also have been the specific wish of Princess Anne. (As female-line grandchildren of the Sovereign, Princess Anne's children were never eligible for the style "Royal Highness" or the title "Prince/Princess" under the terms of George V's letters patent of 1917). If Phillips held a peerage, however, his children with Princess Anne would have been entitled to be addressed as "Lord" or "Lady" and not merely "Mr." or "Miss." In the case of the Queen's sister, Princess Margaret, her ex-husband, Anthony Armstrong-Jones, became the Earl of Snowdon upon marriage, with the subsidiary title, Viscount Linley. As a result, Jones' son, David, is entitled to be addressed as "Viscount Linley", and David's son, Charles, is addressed "The Honourable".

Rumours of a stormy relationship were rife, and their home life at Gatcombe Park was the subject of much unwanted media attention throughout their marriage. Several sources, including Nicholas Davies' book 'Queen Elizabeth II: A Woman Who Is Not Amused' have attempted to cast doubt on whether Phillips fathered his daughter Zara. In 1992, Phillips and the Princess Royal were divorced.

Extramarital affair

In August 1985 Phillips fathered a daughter, Felicity, as a result of an extramarital affair with New Zealand art teacher Heather Tonkin. Phillips was confirmed as the father as a result of DNA testing during a paternity suit in 1991.

On 1 February 1997, Phillips married Sandy Pflueger, an American dressage rider. The couple have a daughter named Stephanie, born October 2, 1997.

Titles, styles, honours and arms

Honours
- **CVO**: Commander of the Royal Victorian Order
- **ADC(P)**: Personal Aide-de-Camp to the Queen

Military
- **Captain** (Retired)

Source (edited): "http://en.wikipedia.org/wiki/Mark_Phillips"

Mary Gordon-Watson

Mary Gordon-Watson (born 3 April 1948) is a British equestrian, World champion, Olympic champion and European champion. She won a team gold medal in *eventing* at the 1972 Summer Olympics in Munich, and finished fourth in individual eventing. She became European champion in 1969 and in 1971, and World champion in 1970.

Source (edited): "http://en.wikipedia.org/wiki/Mary_Gordon-Watson"

Mary King (equestrian)

Mary Elizabeth King (née Thomson, born 8 June 1961) is a British Olympic equestrian sportswoman who has represented Great Britain at five Olympics from 1992 to 2008, winning one silver and one bronze medal in the team eventing. She has won two gold and one silver medal in the World Equestrian Games team eventing and four team gold medals at the European Eventing Championships along with one bronze and one silver medal in the individual event. Nationally, she was the British Open Champion in 1990, 1991 & 1996 and won the CCI four star Badminton Horse Trials in 1992 & 2000, and the CCI four star Burghley Horse Trials in 1996.

Early life

King was born in Newark-on-Trent. Her father, Lieutenant-Commander M D H Thomson was a naval officer who suffered for the rest of his life from the consequences of a motorcycle accident that happened before Mary was born. Latterly he took the position of verger in Salcombe Regis parish church. He died in 2000. Her mother Patricia Gillian (Jill) continues the role of verger at the church. Mary also has an elder brother Simon Francis bennett Thomson

She attended Manor House Independent School (Honiton), Kings Grammar School (Ottery St Mary) and Evendine Court School of Domestic Economy (Cordon Bleu) (Malvern).

She did not grow up in a horsey family, but became fascinated by the vicar's pony, and eventually, aged 6, she persuaded her mother to lead her around the lanes on it. After that, she rode everything she could, even a donkey, and realised that she wanted to become a professional rider. It was not until she went to watch the Badminton Horse Trials, aged 11, with Axe Vale Pony Club, that she realised she wanted to become a professional three-day-event rider.

After school, she went to work for Sheila Willcox, a former European Champion, where she learned everything, from breaking in and producing young horses, to top class stable management.

A longing to travel took her to Zermatt where she worked as a chalet girl and which she described as being *"great fun and a doddle after working in the yard"*. Subsequently she joined the tall ship, Sir Winston Churchill, first as a trainee, then as a watch leader, before returning to set up her own stables.

King converted a couple of cow sheds in a disused farmyard near her home and looked after other people's horses, gave riding lessons and bought and sold horses. To supplement her income, she cleaned houses, cooked, kept gardens tidy for people and delivered meat for the local butcher.

Funding proved even more difficult in 1988 when she started competing professionally, requiring her to sell horses which had proven successful. This changed, when after being offered good money for Divers Rock, a horse on which she had achieved 7th place at Badminton, she turned the offer down commenting *"I'd rather be famous than rich."* It proved to be the right decision because she secured her first sponsorship deal on the back of her success.

Equestrian career

King went to her first Badminton in 1985, finishing in seventh place, and finally won the event in 1992 with her horse, King William. She later won the event again in 2000 with Star Appeal.

In 2001, whilst exercising horses at her home, she had a fall which broke her neck. However, less than a year later she was back at the top of the sport recording top ten placings at major international events including a 3rd placing at Burghley Four Star on her great campaigner King Solomon III.

She has won six team gold medals at World Equestrian Games and European Championships. She has been British Champion four times, more than anyone to date. King has also represented Britain in five Olympic Games: 1992, 1996, 2000, 2004 and 2008. She won bronze with the 2008 Olympic team with Call Again Cavalier.

She married Alan King (known as David King) in 1995 and they and their two children, Emily and Freddie, live in Salcombe Regis, Devon.

Horses

Current

Mary King on King's Gem at the 2007 Blenheim Horse Trials

- Imperial Cavalier (by Cavalier Royale out of Gene Pool)
- Apache Sauce (by Endoli out of Saucy Secret)
- Fernhill Urco (by Corrado-Fly out of Orli)
- King Albert (by Mayhill out of Kings Gem)
- Kings Temptress (by Primitive Rising out of Kings Mistress)
- Cavalier Venture (by Newmarket Venture out of Newmarket Ratr Cavalier)

Former

- Call Again Cavalier 1992-2008 (by Cavalier Royale out of My Woodlands Lady VII, half brother to Cashel Bay and Imperial Cavalier) - put down on 30 November 2008 after sustaining a broken leg at the Express Eventing International Cup, Cardiff.
- Cashel Bay (by Cavalier Royale) Now competing with John Paul Sheffield.
- King William 1983-2002 (by Nickel King) - put down due to cut hoof and pastern (retired with Annie collings)
- Butterboy - first pony
- King Kong (retired to hunting field)
- King Samuel(sold)
- Star Appeal (won Badminton CCI 4* 2000) then retired to former groom Annie Collings
- King Boris (retired to Paula Lee)
- King Basil (sold)
- King Solomon (won Olympic medal)
- King Cuthbert (retired to Annie Collings)
- King Humphrey
- King Max
- Diver's Rock (competed him at her first ever Badminton in 1985, placed 7th)
- King's Mistress (dam to many of Mary's current event horses)

Bred

- Kings Fancy (by Rock King out of Kings Mistress, full sister to Kings Gem) - Now competing with eventer Laura Shears.
- Kings Gem (by Rock King out of Kings Mistress, full sister to Kings Fancy) - Now competing with eventer Gemma Tattersall.
- Kings Temptress (by Primitive Rising out of Kings Mistress)
- Kings Rock (by Primitive Rising out of Kings Fancy)- Now competing with eventer Georgie Spence.
- Kings Command (by Primitive Rising out of Kings Mistress, half brother to Kings Fancy, Kings Gem, and full brother to Kings Temptress) Now competing with Charlotte Martin.
- King Albert (by Mayhill out of Kings Gem)
- King Casper, renamed Everys King for 2010 season. (By Med Night Mahout out of Kings Temptress) Ridden by Emily King, Mary's daughter.

Achievements

Mary King and Kings Temptress at the Discovery Valley during the cross country phase of Burghley Horse Trials 2009.

Mary King and Apache Sauce jump the Lake during the cross-country phase of Badminton Horse Trials 2008.

2011
- 3rd Badminton Horse Trials International CCI **** (Imperial Cavalier)
- 1st Rolex Kentucky Three Day CCI **** (Kings Temptress)
- 2nd Rolex Kentucky Three Day CCI **** (Fernhill Urco)

2010
- 4th Badminton Horse Trials International CCI **** (Imperial Cavalier)
- Team Gold At FEI World Equestrian Games, Kentucky (Imperial Cavalier)
- 6th World Games Kentucky (Imperial Cavalier)

2009
- 12th Burghley Horse Trials CCI**** (Apache Sauce)
- 18th Burghley Horse Trials CCI**** (Kings Temptress)
- 2nd Hartpury CIC*** (Apache Sauce)
- 7th Gatcombe CIC***W (Kings Temptress)
- 4th Luhmühlen Horse Trials CCI**** (Kings Temptress)
- 5th Barbury Castle CIC*** (Apache Sauce)
- 4th Aachen CICO*** (Imperial Cavalier)
- 3rd Tattersalls CIC***W (Imperial Cavalier)
- 6th Tattersalls CIC*** (Fernhill Urco)

2008
- 8th Pau CCI**** (Call Again Cavalier)
- 3rd Burghley Horse Trials CCI**** (Imperial Cavalier)
- 4th Burghley Horse Trials CCI**** (Apache Sauce)
- Team Bronze - Beijing Olympics (Call Again Cavalier)
- 8th Barbury International CIC *** (Call Again Cavalier)
- 2nd Bramham International CCI *** (Kings Fancy)
- 8th Saumur International CCI *** (Kings Gem)
- 5th Chatsworth International CIC *** (Kings Temptress)
- 11th Badminton International CCI **** (Apache Sauce)
- 2nd Belton Park International CIC *** (Imperial Cavalier)
- 3rd Burnham Market International CIC *** (Apache Sauce)

2007
- 1st British Open Championships, Gatcombe Park (Call Again Cavalier)
- 2nd European Three Day Eventing Championships (Call Again Cavalier)
- Team Gold - European Three Day Eventing

2005
- 7th Dartfield CCI ** (Apache Sauce)
- 8th Barbury Castle CIC *** (Call Again Cavalier)
- 3rd Blair Castle CCI * (Kings Gem)
- 4th Burghley CCI **** (Call Again Cavalier)

2004
- 20th Athens Olympics
- Team Silver - Athens Olympics

2003
- 5th European Championships, Punchestown, Ireland (King Solomon III)
- 3rd British Open Championships, Gatcombe Park (King Solomon III)
- 10th Bramham CCI *** (King George II)
- 4th Badminton CCI **** (King Solomon III)

2002
- 5th Boekelo CCIO *** (Ryan V)
- 3rd Burghley CCI **** (King Solomon III)
- 2nd Thirlestane Castle CIC ** (King Solomon III)
- 10th Thirlestane Castle CIC ** (King George II)
- 5th Punchestown CCIO *** (Ryan V)
- 4th Chatsworth CIC *** (King Solomon III)

2001
- 5th Punchestown CCI *** (Ryan V)
- 4th Burghley CCI **** (King Solomon III)
- 2nd Thirlestane CIC ** (King

Richard)

2000
- 7th Olympic Games (Individual Competition), Sydney, Australia (Star Appeal)
- 1st Badminton CCI **** (Star Appeal)

1999
- 5th Burghley CCI **** (King Solomon III)
- 3rd Blair Castle CCI * (King Richard)

1997
- 1st Achselschwang CCI *** (King Solomon III)
- 3rd Blenheim CCI *** (King William)
- 8th and Team gold European Open Championships, Burghley (Star Appeal)
- 3rd Scottish Open Championships, Thirlestane Castle (King Solomon III)
- 2nd British Open Championships (National Champion), Gatcombe Park (King Solomon III)
- 3rd British Open Championships, Gatcombe Park (Star Appeal)
- 1st Chantilly CIC ** (King William)
- 6th Punchestown CCI *** (King William)
- 2nd Badminton CCI **** (Star Appeal)
- 1st Saumur CCI *** (King Solomon III)

1996
- 1st Blenheim CCI *** (King Solomon III)
- 1st Burghley CCI **** (Star Appeal)
- 1st British Open Championships (National Champion), Gatcombe Park (King William)
- 2nd British Open Championships, Gatcombe Park (King Solomon III)
- 1st Scottish Open Championships, Thirlestane Castle (Star Appeal)
- 1st Ladies Advanced, Thirlestane Castle (King Solomon III)
- 12th Olympic Games (Individual), Atlanta, USA (King William)

1995
- Team gold and Individual bronze European Championships, Pratoni del Vivaro, Italy (King William)
- 1st Scottish Open Championships, Thirlestane Castle (King William)
- 2nd Scottish Open Championships, Thirlestane Castle (Star Appeal)
- 2nd British Open Championships, Gatcombe Park (Star Appeal)
- 1st Punchestown CCI *** (Star Appeal)

1994
- 2nd Le Lion d'Angers CCI *** (King Solomon III)
- 2nd Burghley CCI **** (King Kong)
- 4th Burghley CCI **** 1994 (Star Appeal)
- 10th British Open Championships, Gatcombe Park (Star Appeal)
- 4th and Team gold World Equestrian Games, The Hague, Holland (King William)

1993
- 2nd Punchestown CCI *** (Star Appeal)

1992
- 3rd Olympic Games, Barcelona, Spain (King William)
- 2nd FEI Continental Cup Final, Pratoni del Vivaro, Italy (King Samuel)
- 1st Windsor CCI ** (King Kong)
- 1st Badminton CCI **** (King William)

1991
- 1st Loughanmore CCI ** (King Alfred)
- Team gold European Championships, Punchestown, Ireland (King William)
- 1st British Open Championships, Gatcombe Park (King William)
- 1st Osberton CCN (King Kong)

1990
- 2nd Burghley CCI **** (King Cuthbert)
- 4th Burghley CCI **** (King Boris)
- 9th Blenheim CCI *** (King William)
- 1st British Open Championships, Gatcombe Park (King Boris)
- 6th Bramham CCI *** (King William)
- 3rd Badminton CCI **** (King Boris)
- 8th Badminton CCI **** (King Cuthbert)

1989
- 5th Le Lion d'Angers CCI *** (King William)
- 2nd Rotherfield Park CCI *** (King Cuthbert)
- 1st Windsor 3DE (King Max)
- 2nd Badminton CCI **** (King Boris)

1988
- 1st Breda CCI ** (King Max)
- 2nd Bramham CCI *** (King Cuthbert)
- 1st Osberton 3DE (King Samuel)

1987
- 15th Burghley CCI **** (King Boris)
- 2nd Windsor 3DE (King Arthur)

1986
- 1st Osberton 3DE (King Arthur)
- 4th Breda CCI ** (King Boris)
- 1st Bramham CCI *** (King Cuthbert)
- 2nd Bramham CCI *** (Silverstone)

1985
- 7th Badminton CCI **** (Divers Rock)

1984
- 6th Boekelo CCI *** (Divers Rock)

Source (edited): "http://en.wikipedia.org/wiki/Mary_King_(equestrian)"

Michael Whitaker

Michael Whitaker (born April 17, 1960) is a British Olympic equestrian rider, who competes in the sport of show jumping.

Biography

Younger brother of John Whitaker, Michael Whitaker began competing on ponies at the age of 7 years. At the age of 16, he made his debut in international competitions and at 20 years in 1980, he became the youngest winner of the famous Hickstead Derby. In September 1993 he took over from his brother John as the world's no.1 show jumping rider.

Major achievements

- 1984: Olympic Games, Los Angeles. Team Silver medal with *Overton Amanda*
- 1985: European Championships, Dinard. Team Gold medal with *Warren Point*
- 1986: World Championships, Aachen. Team Silver medal with *Warren Point*
- 1987: European Championships, St. Gallen. Team Gold Medal with *Overton Amanda*
- 1989: European Championships, Rotterdam. Team Gold Medal and individual silver medal with *Mon Santa*
- 1990: World Equestrian Games, Stockholm. Team Bronze medal with *Mon Santa*
- 1991: European Championships, La Baule. Team Silver medal with *Mon Santa*
- 1993: European Championships, Gijon. Team Silver medal and individual bronze with *Midnight Madness*
- 1994: World Cup Final, 's-Hertogenbosch. 3rd place with *MidMadness*
- 1995: European Championships, St. Gallen. Silver medals in team and individual with *Two Step*
- 1997: European Championships, Mannheim. Team Bronze Medal with *Ashley*
- 2001: World Cup Final, Gothenburg. 3rd place with *Handel II*
- 2005: World Cup Final, Las Vegas 2nd place with *Portofino 63*
- 2007: European Championships, Mannheim. Team Bronze Medal with *Portofino 63*

Source (edited): "http://en.wikipedia.org/wiki/Michael_Whitaker"

Nick Skelton

Nicholas "Nick" Skelton (born 30 December 1957 in Bedworth, Warwickshire) is a British Showjumper with over 30 years experience.

Biography

He began his riding career at Ted and Liz Edgar's showjumping yard. His first pony, a Welsh Mountain, was called Oxo. He broke his neck in September 2000 which could easily have ended his show jumping career, but after retiring in 2001 he recovered and began competing again om 2002. Skelton won the British Open title in 2004 at the British Open Show Jumping Championships. His current competition horses are owned by Beverley Widdowson. He has written an autobiography, and will soon publish an updated version. Nick has two sons, Harry and Daniel, who both are very active in Horse Racing.

In 2010, Skelton travelled to Hamburg for the second leg of the Global Champions Tour. On day 1 he finished second to Ireland's Denis Lynch in the 1m55 'Mercedes-Benz Championat of Hamburg' with *Carlo*. On day 2 he took the honours in the 1m50 one-round competition with *Unique XVII* to take the €5000 first prize.

Major achievements

He has had many successes with horses such as Maybe, St. James, Apollo, Dollar Girl and Arko. Skelton has ridden on over 144 Nations Cups teams (1978–2007). He has won various medals both as an individual and as part of the teams in the Olympics, World Championships and European Championships between 1980 and 1998.

- Alternative Olympic Games
  - 1980: Rotterdam. Team Silver medal with *Maybe*
- World championships
  - 1982: Dublin. Team Bronze medal with *If Ever*
  - 1986: Aachen. Team Silver medal and individual Bronze medal with *Apollo*
  - 1990: Stockholm. Team Bronze medal with *Grand Slam*
  - 1998: Rome. Team Bronze medal with *Hopes are High*
- European Championships
  - 1985: Dinard. Team Gold medal and individual 4th with *St. James*
  - 1987: St. Gallen. Team Gold medal and individual Bronze medal with *Apollo*
  - 1989: Rotterdam. Team Gold medal with *Apollo*
  - 1991: La Baule. Team Silver medal with *Phoenix Park*
  - 1993: Gijon. Team Silver medal with *Dollar Girl*
  - 1995: St. Gallen. Team Silver medal with *Dollar Girl*
- Junior European Championships
  - 1974: Lucerne. Team Silver medal with *Maybe*
  - 1975: Dornbirn. Team Silver medal and individual Gold medal with *O.K*
- Volvo World Cup Final
  - 1985: Berlin. 2nd with *St James*
  - 1995: Gothenburg. Winner with *Dollar Girl*
  - 1996: Geneva. 3rd with *Dollar Girl*
- Hickstead Derby
  - 1987: Winner with *J Nick*
  - 1988: Winner with *Apollo*
  - 1989: Winner with *Apollo*
- King George V Gold Cup
  - 1984: Winner with *St. James*
  - 1993: Winner with *Limited Edition*
  - 1996: Winner with *Cathleen III*
  - 1999: Winner with *Hopes are High*

Nick Skelton currently holds the British Show Jumping High Jump record, at 7 ft 7in 5/16th (2.32m) set at Olympia in 1978 with *Lastic*.

Horses

Nick Skelton & Arko III, Dublin 2008

The famous horses Maybe, If Ever, Apollo and St. James helped Nick to the become a big name in the showjumping profession, winning many top prizes. Skelton has notably won the Hickstead Derby 3 times. Other horses that Nick has ridden include : Major Wager, Top Gun, Grand Slam, Phoenix Park, Dollar Girl, Limited Edition, Showtime, Tinka's Boy, Hopes are High, Russel and Arko III.

One of his rides, Arko III, is a 1994 16.2 hh Bay Oldenburg Stallion, by Argentinius (Hanoverian), out of Unika (Oldenburg) by Beach Boy (Oldenburg). He was previously ridden by Robert Whitaker. Arko has carried Skelton to several Grand Prix wins, as well as an 11th place finish at the 2004 Athens Olympics. Also another World Class Horse Skelton rode was Russell, owned by John and Lisa Hales, both Arko III and Russell are now both retired and situated at Stud.

Skelton currently rides Big Star, Wotamillion, Unique, Nemo, Transmission and Carlo all of whom are owned by Beverley Widdowson.

Source (edited): "http://en.wikipedia.org/wiki/Nick_Skelton"

Norman Arthur

Lieutenant General **Sir John Norman Stewart Arthur** KCB CVO (born 6 March 1931) was General Officer Commanding in Scotland.

Military career

Educated at Eton College and the Royal Military Academy, Sandhurst, Arthur was commissioned into the Royal Scots Greys in 1951. At the 1960 Summer Olympics in Rome he was part of part of the British equestrian team for the three-day event; he withdrew after the cross-country phase.

He was appointed Commanding Officer of the Royal Scots Dragoon Guards in 1972 and mentioned in despatches for service in Northern Ireland in 1974 during The Troubles. He became Commander of 7th Armed Brigade in 1976.

He went on to be General Officer Commanding 3rd Armoured Division in 1980 and Director of Personal Services (Army) in 1983. He was appointed General Officer Commanding Scotland and Governor of Edinburgh Castle in 1985; he retired in 1988.

In 1996 he became Lord Lieutenant of the Stewartry of Kirkcudbright, Dumfries and Galloway Region.

Family

In 1960 he married Theresa Mary Hopkinson; they went on to have two sons (one of whom died) and a daughter.

Source (edited): "http://en.wikipedia.org/wiki/Norman_Arthur"

Oliver Skeete

Oliver Skeete (born 26 March 1956 in Speightstown, Barbados) is a British showjumper turned reality show contestant and actor.

Biography

One of a family of 10 (4 brothers and 5 sisters), Skeete travelled to England in September 1964 to join his parents who had settled in Acton, West London, and attended local schools to the age of fifteen. On leaving school Skeete qualified as a motor mechanic 3 years later. He worked for a time as a door supervisor at the 'Haven Stables' on Spring Bridge Road in Ealing. His main sporting interest at this time was football and he played for a local youth team. Skeete was first introduced to the world of horses by a chance meeting with a Spanish Countess in a night-club. However, this was not a successful introduction as Skeete was left bruised and embarrassed after being thrown in Hyde Park. After marriage to another lady and two daughters to entertain, Skeete enrolled them at a local riding school. He found that his enthusiasm grew with theirs and decided to chance his luck once more.

Skeete sold the family car to purchase his first horse, and started show jumping in 1992, aged 36. He has competed at most levels except the very top. Skeete intended to represent Barbados at the Olympics in Sydney in 2000, show jumping under the Barbadian flag, but he did not gain the required number of points for qualification.

After Show Jumping

It is fair to state that Skeete attained a level of fame which was out of proportion to his quite modest achievements as a showjumper. This was partly due to his status as a dreadlocked black competitor in the overwhelmingly white, comfortably middle class world of British showjumping, and he used this novelty factor to generate media interest. He has maintained his minor celebrity status since leaving showjumping, appearing in TV shows such as ITV's Celebrity Wrestling and The Mint, Sky One's Brainiac: Science Abuse and Five's The All Star Talent Show and Diet Doctors. He also had a minor role in the Bond movie *Die Another Day*, where he delivered Pierce Brosnan a key to the London Underground "offices" of MI6.

He also had worked on a British film "Clubbing to Death" with Nick Moran, Huey Morgan & Dave Courtney, that was due for release in 2007.

Skeete's autobiography is called "Jumping the Odds: Memoirs of a Rastafarian Showjumper".

As of Mid July 2010 Skeete now works within the haulage industry as a lorry driver for a firm located in Kent. Source (edited): "http://en.wikipedia.org/wiki/Oliver_Skeete"

Pat Smythe

Patricia Rosemary Smythe (22 November 1928 – February 27, 1996), most commonly known as **Pat Smythe**, was one of Britain's premier female showjumpers. She later married in 1960 after the Summer Olympics of the year to childhood friend Sam Koechlin and became **Patricia Koechlin-Smythe**. This meant a move to Switzerland (as he was Swiss) and it was there that many of her books were written. Sam died in 1986 and Pat moved back to the Cotswolds.

Pat's death came due to heart disease when she was 67. She was also the subject of a commemorative plate.

Early years

Pat Smythe was the last of three children, the other two being Dicky and Ronald Smythe. Sadly, Dicky died from pneumonia at the age of 4. Her parents were Eric Hamilton Smythe and Frances Monica Curtoys, who were born in the early 1900s. She lived in London, on the outskirts of Richmond Park. Later she was a boarder at Talbot Heath School in Bournemouth.

Pat nearly died when she was nearly 5 from diphtheria. Although she recovered fully, it meant that she had to learn to walk again. Hardship and suffering were to feature predominantly throughout her professional and personal life. Her father died when she was in her late teens, and her mother when she was 23.

War years

World War II brought times of awkward separation for the family. As well as the usual wartime activity of evacuation and rationing, in early 1940 her father was sent to Biskra in Algeria in search of a respite from his arthritis. Her mother remained in London working for the Red Cross.

During her father's return from North Africa via France, her mother set out to find him. She eventually found him in the town of Aix-les-Bains. Together they managed to get out of France, under enemy fire, on the very last boat leaving Bordeaux just before the Germans occupied the city and the majority of the rest of France.

Pat herself was sent to the Cotswolds (Ferne) for her safety, along with her pony, Pixie. Her brother had been evacuated to Newquay in Devon, where his school had relocated.

It was during that time, whilst getting into an entanglement with several horses, that Pat met the King in the middle of the road. Unaware of who he was, she said to the driver of the car he was travelling in *Shut up! Can't you see I'm trying to get these horses out of the road!*

In early 1941, Pat and her parents relocated to a house in the Cotswolds. Her parents still had to work hard, and things were never easy. The house had to serve as a guesthouse, as well as a family home.

In 1949, after her father's death, Pat and her mother moved again, to Miserden in the Cotswolds.

Ponies/HORSES

Her first ride was on a small pony known as Bubbles. Although he was her brother's pony, she learned to ride on him but outgrew him eventually. After that, her parents bought her a Dartmoor x Arab pony named Pixie. Pixie was later mated with a stallion and gave birth to a filly called Vicky.

Pat's mother used to be sent polo ponies by a friend of the family, Johnny Traill, to break and be schooled for polo playing. Although they were not hers, when she was older, Pat also helped school and break them.

It was not until Pat's relocation to the Cotswolds that her first taste of showjumping came with Finality. After varied success at gymkhanas and numerous injuries which Finality suffered, Pat was able to compete in her first International Show. Eventually she was asked to join the British team with Colonel Harry Llewellyn, Ruby Holland-Martin, Toby Robeson and Brian Butler in 1947. But the partnership with Finality was not to last. She had been lent to the family by Johnny Traill and, due to financial pressure, had to be sold.

Pat's next horse, the grey mare Carmena, came after the parting with Finality. Although Carmena was a talented and successful horse, Pat admitted that she could never feel the same closeness she had had with Finality.

Shortly after Carmena came another mare, Leona. Leona served Pat well until the death of her mother meant that finances became pretty tight. Being the most valuable horse (at the time), Leona had to be sold.

In 1949, Pat acquired her cheapest horse Prince Hal. Bought as a cheap ex-racehorse, he was initially named Fourtowns. He was re-named Prince Hal after a role of Laurence Olivier.

Tosca was Pat's next purchase. She was born in 1945. It was her most successful partnership after Finality, winning many medals and major showjumping prizes of the day. Tosca was one of the ones she most often competed abroad. After Tosca's retirement from showjumping in the mid 1950s, she bred several foals, including Lucia (by Gay Scot, born 1957), Favourita (by Blue Duster, born 1958), Flamenca (by Tambourin, born 1959), Laurella (by Schapiro, born 1960), Prince Igor (by Shapiro born 1961), Chocolate Soldier (her sixth, by either Bitter Sweet or Cortachy, born 1962), Melba (by Pincola, born 1963), Sir John (by Shapiro, born 1964) and a final foal (name unknown, by Three Card Trick). It may have been the case that after 1965, she produced several more foals.

Lucia herself produced a few foals herself which include Titania (by Schapiro, born 1962), Caruso (by Pinicola, born 1963) and Queen of Hearts (by Three Card Trick, born 1965)

Later showjumping horses included Flanagan, Brigadoon, Scorchin, Mr Pollard and Telebrae.
Source (edited): "http://en.wikipedia.org/wiki/Pat_Smythe"

Paul Aloysius Kenna

Brigadier General **Paul Aloysius Kenna** VC DSO (16 August 1862 – 30 August 1915) was an English born British Army officer of Irish descent and recipient of the Victoria Cross (VC), the highest and most prestigious award for gallantry in the face of the enemy that could be awarded to British and British Empire forces.

Background

He was the son of Thomas Kenna, a wealthy stockbroker of Liverpool who was descended from a family of minor gentry from County Meath. Kenna was educated at Stonyhurst College and St. Francis Xavier College in Liverpool - he is honoured in a memorial which can be seen in the main hall of the current college site in Beaconsfield Road, Liverpool. Kenna married Lady Cecil Bertie, daughter of the 7th Earl of Abingdon.

Victoria Cross

Kenna was 36 years old, and a captain in the 21st Lancers (Empress of India's), British Army during the Sudan Campaign when the following deed took place for which he was awarded the VC:

On 2 September 1898, at the Battle of Omdurman, Sudan, when a major of the 21st Lancers was in danger, as his horse had been shot in the charge, Captain Kenna took the major up on his own horse, to a place of safety. After the charge Captain Kenna returned to help Lieutenant De Montmorency who was trying to recover the body of an officer who had been killed.

Olympics

He competed in the 1912 Summer Olympics for Great Britain as a horse rider. He did not finish the Individual eventing (Military) competition, also the British team did not finish the team event. In the individual jumping event he finished 27th.

The 21st Lancers at Omdurman

World War I

He was killed in action at Suvla, Turkey during the Battle of Gallipoli on 30 August 1915, aged 53 and is buried in Lala Baba Cemetery.

His VC is on display in The Queen's Royal Lancers Regimental Museum in Thoresby Park, Nottinghamshire.
Source (edited): "http://en.wikipedia.org/wiki/Paul_Aloysius_Kenna"

Pippa Funnell

Pippa Funnell MBE (born Philippa Rachel Nolan, 7 October 1968) is an equestrian sportswoman, regarded as one of the Eventing's sporting elite. She competes in three-day eventing. In 2003 she became the first person and currently only person to win Eventing's greatest prize, the Rolex Grand Slam of eventing (consecutive wins at Kentucky, Badminton and Burghley.) Her most famous horses are Sir Barnaby, Supreme Rock, Bits and Pieces, Primmore's Pride and Ensign.

Life

Funnell was born in Crowborough, East Sussex in 1968 to Jenny and George Nolan. She grew up in Mark Cross and went to the Mark Cross CE primary school. She attended the independent boarding school Wadhurst College (became Micklefield Wadhurst in the 1990s then Bellerbys in 1997) on *Mayfield Lane* in Wadhurst. Aged 16, she persuaded her parents to allow her to leave school, after which she based herself with Ruth McMullin, establishing one of the sport's most renowned training partnerships. In 2005, Funnell was made an MBE in the Queen's Birthday Honours List.

She lives in Ockley, Surrey with showjumping husband William Funnell. She married him in October 1993 in Uckfield. Following a year apart due to so called marriage difficulties, Pippa and William are back together.

Career

Funnell became *European Young Rider Champion* in 1987 after successfully competing on *Sir Barnaby* at Bialy Bor, Poland. Despite a successful career as a junior and young rider, Pippa at first struggled to establish herself as a senior international. Too often she would put up a brilliant performance in the dressage phase and then throw it away with mistakes on the cross country course. By her own admission she suffered from nerves that were threatening to ruin her career.

Help from sports psychologist Nicky Heath has produced a dramatic change and meant she has become the backbone of the British team. In 1999 she became European Champion at Luhmühlen riding *Supreme Rock* and again on the same horse in 2001 at Pau ("Les Etoiles de Pau" - France). She was a member of the British teams that won silver at the Sydney Olympics in 2000, bronze at the World Equestrian Games in 2002, and silver again at the Athens Olympics of 2004. In addition, Funnell won the individual bronze medal at Athens. (She competed at the Athens Olympics as 'Philippa' rather than 'Pippa' as 'Pipa' in Greek is slang for a sexual act.)

In 2003 she became the first rider ever to complete the Rolex Grand Slam of Eventing by adding the Burghley title to her victories earlier in the year at Lexington and Badminton, to earn a $250,000 bonus from Rolex and a place in the history books. As a result of her phenomenal achievements she was voted Sunday Times Sportswoman of the Year 2003 and was in the top five of the BBC Sports Personality of the Year Awards. She then went to Punchestown in Ireland to defend the individual European title that she had won in 1999 and 2001. Without the great Supreme Rock, on whom she had won her two previous titles, she narrowly failed to make it three in a row, clinching a bronze medal with the inexperienced Walk On Star and helping the British team to win their fifth successive team title. Pippa also finished the year as the number one ranked rider in the world.

In total Funnell has won the Badminton Horse Trials three times: 2002, 2003 and 2005. She has won both the Blenheim venue and Windsor Horse Trials four times as well, the only rider yet to do so.

Recent career

The past two years have been quieter for Funnell in terms of competitive success. Several of her top horses, such as Supreme Rock, Primmores Pride, Viceroy, Walk on Star, Cornerman and Jurassic Rising reached the end of their careers and were retired. Funnell nevertheless remains in the spotlight with Ensign, who narrowly lost an individual medal at the 2005 Europeans and ensured the combination were placed on the shortlist for the 2008 Olympics following a 2nd place at Pau CCI**** in late 2007. Funnell has also kept herself preoccupied with talented youngsters. Already a renowned producer of young horses, having won a record number of Burghley Young Event Horses classes, and numerous medals, she now has an enviable string of young horses poised to place her back in the spotlight, such as Ensign, who she has been touchingly expansive over.

Media Activities and Writing

Funnell has appeared on DVDs produced by Equestrian Vision, including *Pippa Funnell, Road to the Top* and *The Funnell Factor*, and in 2005 wrote her story in *Pippa Funnell: The Autobiography*.

Ubisoft has released a number of horse videogames starring Pippa Funnell. These include *Pippa Funnell* for the Nintendo DS and Game Boy Advance, *Pippa Funnell: Stable Adventure* for the Game Boy Advance, and the PC games *Pippa Funnell: The Stud Farm Inheritance*, *Pippa Funnell: Take the Reins* (also for PlayStation 2), *Pippa Funnell 3: The Golden Stirrups Challenge* (more commonly known as Horsez), and *Pippa Funnell 4: Secrets of the Ranch*. *Pippa Funnell: Ranch Rescue* was released in 2007 on the PlayStation 2 and Nintendo Wii.

Pippa Funnell is also the author of a series of children's books called Tilly's Pony Tails, published by Orion Children's Books in the United Kingdom.

The first two books in the series, *Magic Spirit* and *Red Admiral* were first published in May 2009. The series has now been extended to eighteen titles in all. The first four titles have also been recorded as unabridged audiobooks, read by sports presenter Clare Balding.

The central character, Tilly Redbrow, is an adopted child, who is passionate about everything to do with horses and ponies. In the first book in the series, Magic Spirit, Tilly helps rescue a neglected horse. Tilly discovers that she has a special gift for communicating with horses, and when she helps Magic Spirit, Tilly meets Angela, who owns a stables called Silver Shoe Farm. Angela invites Tilly to spend time at Silver Shoe Farm, learning about riding, training and caring for horses. Tilly soon makes friends at the stables and spends all her free time there. Each title in the series tells a new story about Tilly's adventures with horses and ponies that she comes into contact with, as well as her growing relationship with Magic Spirit. The series is also linked by an unfolding story about Tilly's background and birth, the only clue to which is a bracelet made of horsehair. As well as the fictional story, each title also contains a tips section with expert advice from Pippa Funnell on all aspects of horses and ponies.

Titles of the books

- Magic Spirit: the dream horse (2009) ISBN 9781842557099
- Red Admiral: the racehorse (2009) ISBN 9781842557105
- Rosie: the perfect pony (2009) ISBN 9781842557112
- Samson: the stallion (2009) ISBN 9781842557129
- Lucky Chance: the new foal (2009) ISBN 9781842557136
- Solo: the super star (2010) ISBN 9781842557143
- Pride and Joy: the event horse (2010) ISBN 9781444000818
- Neptune: the heroic horse (2010) ISBN 9781444000825
- Parkview Pickle: the naughty show pony (2010) ISBN 9781444000832
- Nimrod: the circus pony (2010) ISBN 9781444000900
- Moonshadow: the Derby winner (2011) ISBN 9781444000917
- Autumn Glory: the new horse (2011) ISBN 9781444000924
- Goliath: the rescue horse (2011) ISBN 9781444002591
- Buttons: the naughty pony (2011) ISBN 9781444002607
- Rusty: the trustworthy pony (2011) ISBN 9781444002614
- Royal Flame: the police horse (2011) ISBN 9781444002621
- Stripy: the zebra foal (2012) ISBN 9781444002638

- Free Spirit: the mustang (2012) ISBN 9781444002645

Audiobooks, read by Clare Balding
- Magic Spirit (2010) ISBN 9781409111856
- Red Admiral (2010) ISBN 9781409111870
- Rosie (2010) ISBN 9781409123071
- Samson (2010) ISBN 9781409123095

Special editions
Tilly's Horse box (2010) ISBN 9781444001303
Tilly's Pony Tails 1-3 (2010) ISBN 9781444002270
Tilly's Pony Tails Annual 2011 (2010) ISBN 9781444001112

Other books by Pippa Funnell
Pippa Funnell: The Autobiography (2005) ISBN 9780752865195
Ask Pippa (Questions and Answers) (2010) ISBN 9781444002652
Source (edited): "http://en.wikipedia.org/wiki/Pippa_Funnell"

Polly Stockton

Polly Stockton (born 23 October 1973) is a British event rider. Polly is a member of the British World Class Performance squad.

Polly Stockton has enjoyed a successful career as a Young Rider, she won the team gold at the 1994 European Young Rider Championships and was the British National Champion in 1999. At Senior level she won at Blenheim and Windsor in 1998. She was selected to take part in the British team at the World Equestrian Games in Jerez in 2002.

Polly also finished second in Burghley in 2002, 2007 and 2009.

Polly finished fourth in the 2009 British Open Championship.

In September 2009, Polly finished second at the Burghley Horse Trials. Riding Westwood Poser, she rode clear rounds in both cross-country and show jumping phases, moving up from 16th place after the dressage phase.

She is married to British car racing driver Chris Stockton

Polly Stockton is currently riding Benromach, who has high hopes for the future.

Source (edited): "http://en.wikipedia.org/wiki/Polly_Stockton"

R. S. Summerhays

R. S. Summerhays was a British expert and author in equine matters.

Biography

At the age of 32 in 1914, he was appointed by the British War Office as a "Civilian Remount Purchasing Officer", with the duty of purchasing horses for World War I. Later he served as part of the Army Service Corps. In the early 1920s he rode in the three horse endurance tests of 60 miles (97 kilometres) a day for five consecutive days. He then became Managing Director of one of the largest hunting, hacking and pony establishments in the country. Later he became editor of the journal *Riding*, retiring after thirteen years. It was then he published the first of his equine titles.

Other Interests

For over 40 years was a horse show judge as well as serving on the boards of many horse breeding societies. He was also president of the Arab Horse Society. His interests included polo. He was the originator of the Horseman's Sunday and also of the Horse and Pony Breeding and Benefit Fund.

Source (edited): "http://en.wikipedia.org/wiki/R._S._Summerhays"

Richard Fanshawe (equestrian)

Richard Gennys Fanshawe (22 June 1906 – 14 April 1988) was a British horse rider who competed in the 1936 Summer Olympics.

He was born in Kildare and died in Cheltenham.

In 1936 he and his horse *Bowie Knife* won the bronze medal as part of the British eventing team, after finishing 26th in the individual eventing competition.

Source (edited): "http://en.wikipedia.org/wiki/Richard_Fanshawe_(equestrian)"

Richard Walker (equestrian)

This article deals with Richard Walker, English equestrian. For other Richard Walkers, see: Richard Walker.
Richard Walker is best known for being the youngest rider ever to win the Badminton Horse Trials. At 18 years and 247 days, the British-born rode his mount, Pasha, to victory at Badminton in 1969. Although he tried to repeat his success, he never won the event again. However, the pair did go on to be part of the British Eventing Team at the 1969 European Championships (Haras-du-Pin, France), where they won not only the Team Gold, but also the Individual Silver medal.

Source (edited): "http://en.wikipedia.org/wiki/Richard_Walker_(equestrian)"

Sarah Piercy

Sarah Piercy (born c. 1981) is a British wheelchair athlete. At the age of 19 and in her first attempt at the race, she won the 2000 London Marathon women's wheelchair competition after a tire puncture slowed defending champion Tanni Grey-Thompson. She has competed in a further four London Marathons, but has been seeking to compete in the equestrian events in the Paralympics as well. In February, 2009, a local online newspaper noted that her equestrian ambitions were being stymied because local riding stables would not allow her to ride their horses due to concerns related to safety regulations.

Source (edited): "http://en.wikipedia.org/wiki/Sarah_Piercy"

Sheila Willcox

Sheila Willcox is a Britain-born eventer who won many notional and international three-day events, including the Badminton Horse Trials and the European Championships. She won Badminton three consecutive years (1957-1959), and was the first woman rider in the UK to achieve international success.

Born in 1937, Willcox began riding in childhood, and participated in Pony Club. She rode in her first Three-Day with partner High and Mighty, an Arabian/pony cross, in 1955 at the young age of eighteen. Her first ride around Badminton occurred only a year later, where she managed to capture second place. After a few more years of hard work, Willcox won the event with High and Mighty in 1957, leading the competition start to finish. She won the Badminton title again with High and Mighty the next year, with a 22 point lead after dressage, widening to a 47 point lead by the end of the event.

Willcox also competed in the 1957 European Championships with High and Mighty, earning both team and individual gold medals. The partnerships also won a team gold at the 1959 European Championships. However, women were not allowed to ride in the Olympic Three-Day competition at this time, and so she was unable to participate despite her great success. Her mount was sold to Ted Marsh, to be used by the British Team, although High and Mighty was in the end never selected.

Sheila Willcox married, becoming Sheila Waddington, and returned to Badminton in 1959 with her new, and inexperienced, mount Airs and Graces. She won the dressage, but had to go slow cross-country due to the ground conditions. However, a rail down in show jumping by fellow competitor David Somerset allowed her to clinch the win. To this day, she is the only rider to have won Badminton three years running.

Willcox also won Little Badminton in 1964, riding Glenamoy.

Willcox competed successfully for several years, winning eight major titles. However, a fall in 1971 at the Tidworth Horse Trials left her partially paralyzed, and she gave up eventing and focused on dressage. She went on to have great success in this equestrian sport as well, reaching the Grand Prix level on Son and Heir.

Source (edited): "http://en.wikipedia.org/wiki/Sheila_Willcox"

Tim Stockdale

Tim Stockdale (born August 12, 1964) is an English equestrian who competes in the sport of show jumping.

He competes in international competitions and rides a number of horses, owned by both himself and others. He has written a number of books and produced a three part training video titled *Successful Showjumping With Tim Stockdale*.

He was banned from competing with the British Olympic team in 2002 but reinstated in 2004 when the British Olympic Association found that his offense was minor. This made him eligible compete with at the 2004 Athens Olympics, although he did not actually make the team.

Source (edited): "http://en.wikipedia.org/wiki/Tim_Stockdale"

Timothy Grubb

Timothy Grubb (30 May 1954 – 11 May 2010) was a British show jumping champion. In 1984 he participated at the Summer Olympics held in Los Angeles where he won a silver medal in team jumping with the British team.

He died from heart failure in Illinois on 11 May 2010.

Source (edited): "http://en.wikipedia.org/wiki/Timothy_Grubb"

Virginia Leng

Virginia Helen Antoinette Holgate, also known as **Ginny Leng**, (born 2 February 1955 in Malta) was a British equestrian competitor who achieved many notable successes in the 1980's, including winning the Individual European Eventing title on 3 consecutive occasions, 1985, 1987 and 1989, a feat which has never been equalled before or since.

She won several national and international titles, including the European Champion, the Badminton Horse Trials and the Burghley Horse Trials a record five times. Among her mounts were Murphy Himself, Night Cap III, and Priceless, the latter two by the eventing stallion Ben Faerie. Since the 1980s, she has written several books.

Ginny Elliott, as she is now known, remains an avid supporter and contributor to the sport of eventing as she is currently (2009) the manager of the Irish Eventing Team.
Source (edited): "http://en.wikipedia.org/wiki/Virginia_Leng"

Wilfred White (equestrian)

Wilfred White (30 March 1904 – 1995) was an equestrian from the United Kingdom and Olympic champion. He won a gold medal in show jumping with the British team at the 1952 Summer Olympics in Helsinki.

Source (edited): "http://en.wikipedia.org/wiki/Wilfred_White_(equestrian)"

William Fox-Pitt

William Speed Lane Fox-Pitt (born 2 January 1969, Hampstead), known as **William Fox-Pitt**, is an English equestrian. He has had notable successes at the Burghley, Badminton, Blenheim and Bramham Horse Trials. He first won the British Open Championships at Gatcombe Park in 1995 and his career highlights include an Olympic team Silver Medal at the Summer Olympic Games at Athens in 2004 and a Team Gold Medal and Individual Silver medal at the World Equestrian Games at Kentucky in 2010.

Life

Educated at Eton and the University of London, Fox-Pitt began riding at age four, and started eventing at age 15. He was born into an equestrian family, with both parents having ridden around Badminton and Burghley and his siblings having been very successful as well. He holds, with Ginny Elliott and Mark Todd, the record for the most wins (five) at the Burghley Horse Trials; William's victories coming in 1994, 2002, 2005, 2007 and 2008. Additional major wins have been at the Badminton Horse Trials in 2004, at Gatcombe Park in 1995, 2000, 2003 and 2005, and team golds in European Championships in 1995, 1997, 2001, 2003 , 2005 and 2009. He also represented Great Britain at the Atlanta, Athens and Beijing Olympics, winning team silver in Athens and team bronze in Beijing. As of 2006, he was ranked the leading rider in Britain for the sixth year running and 2nd in the world. William is married to Channel 4 Racing presenter Alice Plunkett. They have two sons, Oliver who was born in August 2005 and Thomas, born 15 November 2006. William is a regular columnist in the weekly equestrian magazine, Horse & Hound.

In the Eventing world, one of his best known partnerships is with the horse Tamarillo.

Career highlights

William Fox-Pitt and Idalgo at the Hillside during the cross-country phase of Badminton Horse Trials 2009.

2010
- 1st Rolex Kentucky Three Day CCI **** (Cool Mountain)
- 1st Team Event FEI World Equestrian Games Kentucky (Cool Mountain)

2008

- 1st Burghley Horse Trials CCI **** (Tamarillo)
- 2nd Burghley Horse Trials CCI **** (Ballincoola)
- 3rd Badminton Horse Trials CCI **** (Ballincoola)
- 1st Bramham Horse Trials CCI*** (Navigator)
- 1st Luhmühlen Horse Trials CCI **** (Macchiato)

2007
- 1st Bramham Horse Trials CCI*** (Macchiato)
- 1st Burghley Horse Trials CCI **** (Parkmore Ed)
- 1st Blair CCI*** (Macchiato)
- 5th Burghley Horse Trials CCI **** (Ballincoola)

2006
- 9th Badminton Horse Trials CCI **** (Ballincoola)
- 11th Luhmühlen Horse Trials CCI **** (Birthday Night)
- 1st Hartpary CCI*** (Moon Man)
- 15th Aachen WEG **** (Tamarillo)
- 3rd Blenheim Horse Trials CCI*** (Parkmore Ed)
- 6th Burghley Horse Trials CCI **** (Ballincoola)

2005
- 1st Burghley Horse Trials CCI **** (Ballincoola)
- 1st Boekelo Horse Trials CCI*** (Mr. Dumbledore)
- 2nd Badminton Horse Trials CCI **** (Tamarillo)
- 1st Bramham Horse Trials CCI*** (Mr. Dumbledore)
- 2nd Bramham Horse Trials CCI*** (Idalgo)
- 1st Gatcombe British Open (Moon Man)
- Team gold and individual silver at the European Championships (Tamarillo)
- Winner of the British Eventing Premier League

2004
- 1st Badminton Horse Trials CCI **** (Tamarillo)
- 4th Rolex Kentucky Three Day CCI **** (Ballincoola)
- 7th Fontainebleau (Stunning)
- Team silver at the Athens Olympics (Tamarillo)

2003
- 5th Le Lion d'Angers (Idalgo)
- 8th Le Lion d'Angers (Igor de Cluis)
- 1st Boekelo (Tom Cruise)
- Team gold and 8th individual European Championships, Punchestown, Ireland (Moon Man)
- 1st CIC World Cup Qualifier, Thirlestane Castle (Stunning)
- 1st British Open Championships, Gatcombe Park (Stunning)
- 2nd British Open Championships, Gatcombe Park (Moon Man)
- 1st British Intermediate Championships, Gatcombe Park (Tom Cruise II)
- 1st Luhmühlen Horse Trials CIC *** (Tom Cruise II)
- 1st Bramham Horse Trials CCI *** (Wallow)
- 2nd Bramham Horse Trials CCI *** (Ballincoola)
- 7th Saumur (Coastal Ties)
- 1st Chatsworth CIC World Cup Qualifier (Stunning)
- 3rd Rolex Kentucky Three Day CCI **** (Moon Man)

2002
- Team bronze World Equestrian Games, Jerez, Spain (Tamarillo)
- 1st Burghley Horse Trials CCI **** (Highland Lad)
- 7th Burghley Horse Trials CCI **** (Moon Man)
- 4th Boekelo (Stunning)
- 3rd British Open Championships, Gatcombe Park (Moon Man)
- 4th British Open Championships, Gatcombe Park (Stunning)
- 4th Rolex Kentucky Three Day CCI **** (Stunning)
- 2nd Badminton Horse Trials CCI **** (Tamarillo)
- 6th Bramham Horse Trials CCI *** (Highland Lad)
- 8th Bramham Horse Trials CCI *** (Just A Sovereign)

2001
- 5th and Team gold European Champs, Pau, France (Stunning)
- 4th Bonn Roderberg CCIO (Barclay Square)
- 4th Saumur (Stunning)
- 9th Burghley Horse Trials CCI **** (Springleaze Macaroo)

2000
- 1st British Open Champs, Gatcombe Park (Moon Man)
- 1st Blenheim Horse Trials CCI *** (Stunning)
- 2nd Blenheim Horse Trials CCI *** (Tamarillo)

1999
- 2nd Achselschwang (Moon Man)
- 7th Bramham Horse Trials CCI *** (Moon Man)

1997
- Individual silver and Team gold European Open Championships, Burghley (Cosmopolitan II)
- 2nd Scottish Open Championships, Thirlestane Castle (Cosmopolitan II)
- 3rd Badminton Horse Trials CCI **** (Cosmopolitan II)

1996
- 5th Olympic Games Team Competition, Atlanta, USA (Cosmopolitan II)
- 6th Bramham Horse Trials CCI *** (Lismore Lord Charles)
- 5th Boekelo (Mostly Mischief)

1995
- 6th and Team gold European Open Championships, Pratoni del Vivaro, Italy (Cosmopolitan II)
- 1st Bramham Horse Trials CCI *** (Cosmopolitan II)
- 1st British Open Championships, Gatcombe Park (Chaka)
- 6th Blenheim Horse Trials CCI *** (Loch Alan)
- 5th Boekelo (Faerie Diadem)

1994
- 1st Burghley Horse Trials CCI **** (Chaka)
- 2nd Scottish Open Championships, Thirlestane Castle (Chaka)
- 7th Punchestown (Thomastown)
- 2nd British Open Championships, Gatcombe Park (Chaka)

1993
- 7th Badminton Horse Trials CCI **** (Chaka)

1990
- 4th and Team gold Young Rider European Championships (Steadfast)
- 3rd Young Rider National Championships (Faerie Sovereign)

1989

- Individual bronze and Team silver Young Rider European Championships, Achselschwang, Germany

1988
- 4th and Team gold Young Rider European Championships, Zonhoven, Belgium (Steadfast)

1987
- Individual silver Junior European Championships, Pratoni del Vivaro, Italy (Steadfast)
- 5th Junior National Championships

1985
- 8th Junior National Championships 1985

Source (edited): "http://en.wikipedia.org/wiki/William_Fox-Pitt"

William Funnell

William Funnell with *Billy Birr*, Grand Prix of Eindhoven, Internationaal Concours Hippique Eindhoven (CSI 3*) 2008

William Ross Norman Funnell (born 10 February 1966, Ashford) is a top-class showjumper.

He has been in many Nations Cup teams, but has never ridden in the Olympics. In 2006 he won the Hickstead Derby for the first time since his first attempt at the age of 17, and won it again two years later in 2008. He also won the famous derby of La Baule (France) in 2011. Funnell is married to eventer Pippa Funnell. He married her in October 1993 in Uckfield. They live in Ockley in south Surrey.

Source (edited): "http://en.wikipedia.org/wiki/William_Funnell"

Zara Phillips

Zara Anne Elizabeth Phillips, MBE (born 15 May 1981) is the second child and only daughter of Princess Anne, Princess Royal and her first husband, Captain Mark Phillips. She is the eldest granddaughter of Queen Elizabeth II and Prince Philip, Duke of Edinburgh. At the time of her birth she was sixth in line to succeed her grandmother the Queen. As of the birth of her niece Savannah Phillips in 2010, she is 13th in the line of succession to the thrones of 16 independent countries.

An equestrian, Phillips is the former Eventing World Champion who won the World Championship in Aachen and was voted 2006 BBC Sports Personality of the Year that year by the British viewing public (an award her mother won in 1971). She was appointed a Member of the Order of the British Empire (MBE) in the 2007 New Year's Honours List for her services to equestrianism.

She has an older brother, Peter Phillips, born 15 November 1977, and two half-sisters: Felicity Tonkin, born in 1985 to her father and his former mistress Heather Tonkin; and Stephanie Phillips, born 2 October 1997 from her father's second marriage to Sandy Pflueger.

At the request of their mother, the children of the Princess Royal do not hold any royal title, nor are they entitled to one by right of birth, as they are the grandchildren of a monarch in the female line.

During her time at school, she excelled at many sporting activities and represented her schools in hockey, athletics and gymnastics. She later qualified as a physiotherapist specialising in Equine Physiotherapy from the University of Exeter.

Equestrian

Zara Phillips riding Glenbuck at Badminton Horse Trials 2010

Following in both her parents' footsteps, Phillips is an accomplished equestrian. In June 2003, she announced that she had secured a sponsorship deal with Cantor Index, a leading company in spread betting, to help cover the costs of her equestrian career.

Together with her horse Toytown, she collected individual and team gold medals at the 2005 European Eventing Championship in Blenheim and individual gold and team silver medals at the 2006 FEI World Equestrian Games in Aachen, Germany, making her the reigning Eventing World Champion.

However, despite winning team gold at the 2007 European Eventing Championships in Italy, she failed to defend her own individual title after a problem in the show jumping phase of the competition.

It was announced by the British Olympic Association that Phillips would be riding Toytown as one of five riders for the British equestrian team at the Beijing Olympic Games 2008 in Hong Kong. However, an injury sustained by Toytown during training led to her being forced to withdraw from the team. Zara previously missed the 2004 Summer Olympics in Athens when Toytown suffered a similar injury during training.

On 25 October 2008, she fell from her horse, Tsunami II, at the 15th fence of a cross-country event at Pau, France, and broke her right collarbone. The horse had broken its neck after it had tipped over the hedge and so had to be put down.

As the eldest granddaughter of Queen Elizabeth II, Phillips supports many charitable causes. In 2003, she and Princess Anne took part in the first UK double ship-naming ceremony in Southampton. Princess Anne named the P&O Cruises liner *Oceana*, and Phillips named its sister ship *Adonia*.

She frequently attends various events for charity and has taken to supporting certain causes herself, mainly for spinal injuries, equestrian charities and children's causes. In 2005, she auctioned one of her evening gowns (worn at the London premiere of the film *Seabiscuit*) to raise money for tsunami relief. She also undertook a visit to New Zealand in her role as patron of The Catwalk Trust. From 1998 to 2005 she served as the president of Club 16-24, a group which encourages young people to take an interest in racing. She is linked to INSPIRE, the Salisbury based medical research charity which helps to improve the quality of life of people with spinal cord injuries, and Sargent Cancer Care for Children, the UK's leading children's cancer charity.

She appears at events for The Caudwell Charitable Trust, which is targeted at children with special needs, disabilities and serious illnesses. She has continued her family's long patronage of Great Ormond Street Hospital for Children and has visited on many occasions. In 2006, she took part in a special charity day for Cantor Index, whose staff were killed in the 11 September 2001 attacks. In 2007, she became patron of the Mark Davies Injured Riders Fund. To help with Sport Relief 2008, she posed for her first official royal portrait by artist Jack Vettriano. In 2009, she attended a celebrity poker tournament in Monaco in aid of Darfur, Sudan. In September 2010, she attended the 2012 London Olympic Ball alongside cousin Prince Harry of Wales. In October of the same year she will attend another celebrity poker tournament, this time in London, in aid of Cancer Research UK, of which she is Royal Patron.

Relationships

Phillips' often stormy relationship with former fiancé and National Hunt jockey Richard Johnson attracted the attention of the British paparazzi, and the couple's split in November 2003 became front page news.

On 21 December 2010, Buckingham Palace announced her engagement to rugby union player Mike Tindall, who plays for Premiership side Gloucester and the England national team. She lives with Tindall at their home in Gloucestershire. The couple met during England's Rugby World Cup-winning campaign in Australia in 2003. The wedding will be held on 30 July 2011 at the Canongate Kirk in Edinburgh, Scotland.

Clothing design

In 2009 it was announced that Phillips would be designing her own range of equestrian clothing for Musto Outdoor Clothing. The range is named ZP176 after the team number Zara was given when she first represented her country. The range was officially launched in July 2010.

Source (edited): "http://en.wikipedia.org/wiki/Zara_Phillips"

All England Jumping Course at Hickstead

Competitor on Derby course, with Derby bank in the background

The **All England Jumping Course at Hickstead**, known widely as **Hickstead** is an equestrian sport centre in West Sussex, England, principally known for its showjumping activities, where it hosts two international level competitions, the British Jumping Derby and the Royal International Horse Show. The course was the first permanent showground for equestrian sport in the country.

The venue has more recently expanded its operations to include other equestrian sports including dressage and arena polo as well as hosting functions and conferences all year round.

It is located adjacent to the hamlet of Hickstead, to the west of Burgess Hill and next to the main A23 road from London to Brighton.

History

The All England Jumping venue was opened by Douglas Bunn, a multi-millionaire former barrister who made his money running a caravan business. Bunn purchased a site known as Hickstead Place with the intention of creating a facility to match those in the United States and continental Europe. The venue opened in 1960. It now has six arenas, permanent seating for over 5,000 spectators and 26 corporate hospitality suites. It has hosted the 1965 Ladies World Championships, the 1974 World Championships and several European Show Jumping Championships.

British Jumping Derby

This four-day, action-packed event attracts 20,000 spectators a year, who come to watch the skill, bravery and precision of the national and international show jumpers competing for coveted trophies (and substantial prize money).

A highlight of the meeting is the British Jumping Derby, a 1,195-metre course with tricky jumps including he aptly-named Devil's Dyke – three fences in short succession with a water-filled ditch in the middle and the difficult Derby Bank, a jump with 3 ft 5 in (1.04 m) rails on top and a 10 ft 6 in (3.20 m) slope down the front.

The DFS British Jumping Derby is one of those events a bit like the Grand National where its not just the runners and riders that make the headlines but the course itself. Its an iconic showjumping contest, the like of which you won't find anywhere else in the world, no other course asks this much of a test of horse and rider and no other course creates this type of drama.

—Clare Balding, *BBC Sport*

Royal International Horse Show

The Royal International Horse Show is the official horse show of the British Horse Society and consists of both showing and showjumping events. The event is held during July each year.

Other events

1993 saw the establishment of a dressage arena and dressage programme known as **Dressage at Hickstead**. In 1998 it hosted Junior and Young Rider European Dressage Championships.

2006 saw the creation of the All England Polo Club. Arena (winter) Polo is played on a 100m x 50m purpose built all weather arena

Source (edited): "http://en.wikipedia.org/wiki/All_England_Jumping_Course_at_Hickstead"

Badminton Horse Trials

Paul Tapner celebrates after winning Badminton Horse Trials 2010 on Inonothing.

Gemma Tattersall and Jesters Quest jump the Open Ditch during the cross-country phase of Badminton Horse Trials 2007.

The **Badminton Horse Trials** is a three-day event, one of only six annual Concours Complet International (CCI) Four Star **** events as classified by the Fédération Équestre Internationale (FEI), which takes place in April or May each year in the park of Badminton House, the seat of the Dukes of Beaufort in Gloucestershire, England.

History

Badminton was first held in 1949 by the 10th Duke of Beaufort in order to let British riders train for future international events and was advertised as "*the most important horse event in Britain*". It was the second three day event held in Britain, with the first being its inspiration - the 1948 Olympics. The first Badminton had 22 horses from Britain and Ireland start, and was won by Golden Willow. Eight of the 22 starters failed to complete the cross-country course. Badminton was the home of the first European Championship in 1953, and was won by Major Laurence Rook on Starlight XV. In 1955, Badminton moved to Windsor Castle for a year, at the invitation of the Queen, in order to hold the second European Championships. Badminton was first televised in 1956. In 1959, it was decided to hold Badminton in two sections, called the Great and Little Badminton, due to the popularity of the event and the number of entries. The horses in the two sections jumped the same fences, but were separated into the two divisions based on their money winnings. This graded approach was abandoned after the 1965 event. In 1989, the current director & course-designer Hugh Thomas, who rode in the 1976 Montreal Olympics, took over from Frank Weldon, a former winner, who is credited with bringing the event to the pinnacle it's at today.

Today's Badminton is held in a 6 square kilometre (1500 acre) area Badminton Park, where the car parks, trade-stands, arena and cross country courses are located.

Badminton has been forced to cancel on several occasions for various reasons. In 1966, 1975 and 1987 the event was cancelled completely and in 1963 was downgraded to a one-day event due to bad weather. In 2001 it was cancelled due to foot and mouth disease.

Between 1961 and 1991, Badminton was sponsored by Whitbread, one of the longest sponsorships for any sport. In 1992, Mitsubishi Motors took over sponsorship and recently renewed their deal until 2011.

Status

Together with the four-star rated Rolex Kentucky Three Day and the Burghley Horse Trials, Badminton forms the Rolex Grand Slam of Eventing. The only person ever to win the Grand Slam is Pippa Funnell. Andrew Hoy (Aus) nearly took the title in 2007 but lost it when he had a pole down at Burghley. The remaining CCI**** rated events are the Luhmühlen Horse Trials, the Australian International Three Day Event and the Stars of Pau. It is also now part of the HSBC FEI Classics—a points-based system containing the CCI**** events.

The cross country day at Badminton attracts crowds of up to a quarter of a million, which are the largest for any paid-entry sport event in the United Kingdom, and the second largest in the world (after the Indianapolis 500).

Winners

2011 winners Mark Todd and NZB Land Vision at the Quarry during the cross-country phase.

Paul Tapner and Inonothing, the winning combination at Badminton Horse Trials 2010, at The Lake during the cross-country phase.

Oliver Townend and Flint Curtis, the winning combination at Badminton Horse Trials 2009, at the Hillside during the cross-country phase.

The event has been won by the following people and horses:

- 1949 John Shedden : Golden Willow
- 1950 Tony Collins : Remus
- 1951 Hans Schwarzenbach : Vae Victis
- 1952 Mark Darley : Emily Little
- 1953 Laurence Rook : Starlight
- 1954 Margaret Hough : Bambi V
- 1955 Frank Weldon : Kilbarry *(Event held at Windsor)*
- 1956 Frank Weldon : Kilbarry
- 1957 Sheila Waddington (Sheila Willcox) : High and Mighty
- 1958 Sheila Waddington (Sheila Willcox) : High and Mighty
- 1959 Sheila Waddington (Sheila Willcox) : Airs and Graces
- 1960 Bill Roycroft : Our Solo
- 1961 Laurie Morgan : Salad Days
- 1962 Anneli Drummond-Hay : Merely-a-Monarch
- 1963: *Event downgraded to 1 day event due to bad weather.*
- 1964 James Templer : M'Lord Connolly
- 1965 Eddie Boylan : Durlas Eile
- 1966: *Event cancelled due to bad weather.*
- 1967 Celia Ross-Taylor : Jonathan
- 1968 Jane Holderness-Roddam (Jane Bullen) : Our Nobby
- 1969 Richard Walker : Pasha
- 1970 Richard Meade : The Poacher
- 1971 Mark Phillips : Great Ovation
- 1972 Mark Phillips : Great Ovation
- 1973 Lucinda Green (Lucinda Prior-Palmer) : Be Fair
- 1974 Mark Phillips : Colombus
- 1975: *Event cancelled due to bad weather.*
- 1976 Lucinda Green (Lucinda Prior-Palmer) : Wide Awake
- 1977 Lucinda Green (Lucinda Prior-Palmer) : George
- 1978 Jane Holderness-Roddam (Jane Bullen) : Warrior
- 1979 Lucinda Green (Lucinda Prior-Palmer) : Killaire
- 1980 Mark Todd : Southern Comfort III
- 1981 Mark Phillips : Lincoln
- 1982 Richard Meade : Speculator III
- 1983 Lucinda Green (Prior-Palmer) : Regal Realm
- 1984 Lucinda Green (Prior-Palmer) : Beagle Bay
- 1985 Ginny Leng (Ginny Holgate) : Priceless
- 1986 Ian Stark : Sir Wattie
- 1987: *Event cancelled due to bad weather.*
- 1988 Ian Stark : Sir Wattie *(Stark also came second on Glenburnie)*
- 1989 Ginny Leng (Ginny Holgate) : Master Craftsman
- 1990 Nicola Coe : Middle Road
- 1991 Rodney Powell : Irishman II,
- 1992 Mary King : King William
- 1993 Ginny Leng (Ginny Holgate) : Welton Houdini
- 1994 Mark Todd : Horton Point
- 1995 Bruce Davidson : Eagle Lion
- 1996 Mark Todd : Bertie Blunt
- 1997 David O'Connor : Custom Made
- 1998 Chris Bartle : Word Perfect II
- 1999 Ian Stark : Jaybee
- 2000 Mary King : Star Appeal
- 2001: *Event cancelled due to UK foot and mouth epidemic.*
- 2002 Pippa Funnell : Supreme Rock
- 2003 Pippa Funnell : Supreme Rock
- 2004 William Fox-Pitt : Tamarillo
- 2005 Pippa Funnell : Primmore's Pride
- 2006 Andrew Hoy : Moonfleet
- 2007 Lucinda Fredericks : Headley Britannia
- 2008 Nicolas Touzaint : Hildago de L'Ile
- 2009 Oliver Townend : Flint Curtis
- 2010 Paul Tapner : Inonothing
- 2011 Mark Todd : NZB Land Vision

Casualties

2007
- Skwal ridden by Andrew Downes died of a suspected heart attack in the finishing ring
- Icare d'Auzay ridden by Jean-Lou Bigot died after a fence flag marker pole pierced an artery

2010
- Desert Island ridden by Louisa

Lockwood, euthanised after breaking a fetlock

Criticism

In 2007, after a long period without rain, the ground was considered to be too hard, resulting in 22 withdrawals.
Source (edited): "http://en.wikipedia.org/wiki/Badminton_Horse_Trials"

Blenheim Horse Trials

British rider and 1996 Blenheim-winner Mary King at the 2007 Blenheim Horse Trials

The **Blenheim Horse Trials** is an annual international three day event held in the park of Blenheim Palace, at Woodstock, England. It is rated CCI*** (the second highest level of eventing).

Blenheim began in 1990, after the three-day event held at Chatsworth was ended. The venue has since become popular both for national and international events, beginning in 1994 with the FEI European Young Rider Championships.

In 2003, Blenheim hosted the Asia-Pacific Championships as a qualifier for the 2004 Athens Olympics. Sixteen nations were represented and several European, World, and Olympic Champions competed. The winner, Pippa Funnell, became the first rider to win three times at the venue. Pippa Funnell won yet again at the 2004 Blenheim Horse Trials, on her stallion, Viceroy.

In 2005, Blemheim hosted the European Eventing Championship.

Past Winners of Blenheim

- **1990** Lucinda Murray (now Mrs Fredericks)/Just Jeremy (GBR)
- **1991** Andrew Nicholson/Park Grove (NZL)
- **1992** Rodney Powell/Limmy's Comet (GBR)
- **1993** Pippa Nolan (now Mrs Funnell)/Metronome (GBR)
- **1994** Bruce Davidson/Squelch (USA)
  - Young Rider European Champion: Nina Melkonian/Westphalia/GER
  - Young Rider European Championships Team: GBR
- **1995** Pippa Funnell/Bits And Pieces (GBR)
- **1996** Mary King/King Solomon lll (GBR)
- **1997** Paddy Muir/Archie Brown (GBR)
- **1998** Polly Clark (now Mrs Stockton)/Westlord (GBR)
- **1999** Franck Bourny/Mallard's Treat (FRA)
- **2000** William Fox-Pitt/Stunning (also 2nd on Tamarillo (horse)) (GBR)
- **2001** Kimberly Vinoski (now Ms Severson)/Winsome Adante (USA)
- **2002** Lucinda Fredericks/Headley Britannia (AUS)
- **2003** Pippa Funnell/Jurassic Rising (GBR) (also 3rd on Viceroy ll)
  - Asia-Pacific Champion: Phillip Dutton/Nova Top (AUS)
  - Asia-Pacific Winning Team: Australia
- **2004** Pippa Funnell/Viceroy II
- **2005** European Eventing Championships
  - Zara Phillips and Toytown (GBR) Individual Gold
  - Great Britain Team Gold
- **2006** Daisy Dick/Sprinkbok IV
- **2007** Chris King/The Secret Weapon
- **2008** Cancelled after dressage phase due to poor weather
- **2009** Lucy Wiegersma/Granntevka Prince
- **2010** William Fox-Pitt/Parklane Hawk

Source (edited): "http://en.wikipedia.org/wiki/Blenheim_Horse_Trials"

Bramham Horse Trials

Bramham Horse Trials is one of the UK's premier three day events, taking place every June on the Lane Fox's Bramham Park Estate, near Leeds in Yorkshire. The event attracts an average of 45,000 spectators.

The event first ran in 1974 and now runs as a CCI*** event, attracting top riders and horses, and also incorporates the Under-25 championship and other attractions such as the Winergy Burghley Young Event Horse competition, BSJA showjumping, showing classes and a range of rural attractions and tradestands.

The winner William Fox-Pitt of 2005 also claimed 2nd place, with Mr Dumbledore and Idalgo respectively, as was one of only a few riders to successfully negotiate Sue Benson's stiff cross country track.

Source (edited): "http://en.wikipedia.org/wiki/Bramham_Horse_Trials"

Burghley Horse Trials

A competitor in the 2004 Horse Trials shows good form over the first fence on the cross-country course.

The **Land Rover Burghley Horse Trials** is an annual three day event held at Burghley House near Stamford, Lincolnshire, England, currently in early September. The Land Rover Freelander Burghley Horse Trial is classified by the FEI as one of the six leading three day events in the world (the others being the Badminton Horse Trials, the Rolex Kentucky Three Day, the Adelaide Horse Trials, the Luhmühlen Horse Trials and the Étoiles de Pau). It has competition at CCI**** (four star) level. The prize for first place is currently £50,000. Prize money is given down to 20th place.

Burghley is also one of the three events in the Grand Slam of Eventing.

Run in conjunction with the event since 1990 is the Burghley Young Event Horse final, which judges 4 and 5 year old horses on their potential as future Olympic mounts.

History

Horse trials have been held at Burghley House since 1961 when its owner the 6th Marquess of Exeter, an Olympic gold medallist in athletics and IOC member, heard that a three day event at Harewood House could no longer be held. Since then no other international horse trials site has staged as many championships, a record ten in all including the first World Championship in 1966.

It is the longest continuous running international event. Up to 2006 there have been six course designers: Bill Thomson, M.R.C.V.S. 1961 - 1983, Lt.-Col. Henry Nicoll, D.S.O., O.B.E., 1975, Philip Herbert 1984 - 1988, Capt. Mark Phillips, C.V.O., 1989 - 1996 and 1998 - 2000, Mike Tucker 1997 and 2001, Wolfgang Feld 2002 - 2004 and Capt. Mark Phillips, C.V.O., 2005 -.

Past winners

William Fox-Pitt, here clearing the Cottesmore Leap, has won Burghley five times to date, equalling Mark Todd and Ginny Leng for wins at Burghley.

Winners of the 2010 Burghley Horse Trials, Caroline Powell and Lenamore, at the Dairy Farm during the Cross Country phase.

Oliver Townend and Carousel Quest, the winning combination at Burghley Horse Trials 2009, at the Discovery Valley during the cross country phase.

- 2010 - Caroline Powell on Lenamore
- 2009 - Oliver Townend on Carousel Quest
- 2008 - William Fox-Pitt on Tamarillo
- 2007 - William Fox-Pitt on Parkmore Ed
- 2006 - Lucinda Fredericks on Headley Britannia
- 2005 - William Fox-Pitt on Ballincoola
- 2004 - Andrew Hoy on Moon Fleet
- 2003 - Pippa Funnell on Primmore's Pride
- 2002 - William Fox-Pitt on Highland Lad
- 2001 - Blyth Tait on Ready Teddy
- 2000 - Andrew Nicholson on Mr. Smiffy
- 1999 - Mark Todd on Diamond Hall Red
- 1998 - Blyth Tait on Chesterfield
- 1997 - Mark Todd on Broadcast News
- 1996 - Mary King on Star Appeal
- 1995 - Andrew Nicholson on

Buckley Province
- 1994 - William Fox-Pitt on Chaka
- 1993 - Stephen Bradley on Sassy Reason
- 1992 - Charlotte Hollingsworth on The Cool Customer
- 1991 - Mark Todd on Welton Greylag
- 1990 - Mark Todd on Face the Music
- 1989 - Virginia Leng on Master Craftsman
- 1988 - Jane Thelwell on King's Jester
- 1987 - Mark Todd on Wilton Fair
- 1986 - Virginia Leng (née Holgate) on Murphy Himself
- 1985 - Virginia Holgate on Priceless
- 1984 - Virginia Holgate on Night Cap II
- 1983 - Virginia Holgate on Priceless
- 1982 - Richard Walker on Ryan's Cross
- 1981 - Lucinda Prior-Palmer on Beagle Bay
- 1980 - Richard Walker on John of Gaunt
- 1979 - Andrew Hoy on Davey
- 1978 - Lorna Clarke on Greco
- 1977 - Lucinda Prior-Palmer on George
- 1976 - Jane Holderness-Roddam on Warrior
- 1975 - Aly Pattinson on Carawich
- 1974 - Bruce Davidson on Irish Cap
- 1973 - Captain Mark Phillips on Maid Marion
- 1972 - Janet Hodgson on Larkspur
- 1971 - H.R.H. Princess Anne on Doublet
- 1970 - Judy Bradwell on Don Camillo
- 1969 - Gillian Watson on Shaitan
- 1968 - Sheila Willcox on Fair and Square
- 1967 - Lorna Sutherland on Popadom
- 1966 - Captain Carlos Moratorio on Chalan
- 1965 - Captain J.J. Beale on Victoria Bridge
- 1964 - Richard Meade on Barberry
- 1963 - Captain Harry Freeman-Jackson on St. Finbarr
- 1962 - Captain James Templer on M'Lord Connolly
- 1961 - Anneli Drummond-Hay on Merely-A-Monarch

Source (edited): "http://en.wikipedia.org/wiki/Burghley_Horse_Trials"

Olympia London International Horse Show

Ellen Whitaker with *Ladina B* at the Accenture puissance at 2008 Olympia London International Horse Show

Olympia London International Horse Show is one of the UK's biggest equestrian competitions. Many of the top Show-Jumping riders in the world come here annually as well as some of Britain's finest namely Ellen Whitaker, Tim Stockdale, Ben Maher and many more.

It is held in the Olympia exhibition centre, London.

Olympia celebrated its 100th Anniversary in 2007 as one of Europe's oldest Equine Competitions'. In 2010 it was held as CSI 5*-W (Show Jumping World Cup event) and CDI-W (Dressage World Cup event).

Source (edited): "http://en.wikipedia.org/wiki/Olympia_London_International_Horse_Show"

Royal Windsor Horse Show

The **Royal Windsor Horse Show** is a horse show held annually since 1943 for five days in May or June in Windsor Home Park.

Source (edited): "http://en.wikipedia.org/wiki/Royal_Windsor_Horse_Show"

Tent pegging

Tent pegging (sometimes spelled "tentpegging" or "tent-pegging") is a cavalry sport of ancient origin, and is one of only ten equestrian disciplines officially recognised by the International Federation for Equestrian Sports. Used narrowly, the term refers to a specific mounted game with ground targets. More broadly, it refers to the entire class of mounted cavalry games involving edged weapons on horseback, for which the term "equestrian skill-at-arms" is also used.

An officer of the Indian Army tent pegging with the lance

Essential rules

The specific game of tent pegging has a mounted horseman riding at a gallop and using a sword or a lance to pierce, pick up, and carry away a small ground target (a symbolic tent peg) or a series of small ground targets.

The broader class of tent pegging games also includes ring jousting (in which a galloping rider tries to pass the point of his weapon through a suspended ring); lemon sticking (in which the rider tries to stab or slice a lemon suspended from a cord or sitting on a platform); quintain tilting (in which the rider charges a mannequin mounted on a swivelling or rocking pedestal); and Parthian (i.e., mounted) archery.

A given tent pegging competition's rules specify the size and composition of the target; the number of consecutive targets placed on a course; the dimensions and weight of the sword, lance, or bow; the minimum time in which a course must be covered; and the extent to which a target must be struck, cut, or carried.

Origins

Cavaliers have practised the specific game of tent pegging since at least the 4th century BC, and Asian and later European empires spread the game around the world. As a result, the game's date and location of origin are ambiguous.

In all accounts, the competitive sport evolved out of cavalry training exercises designed to develop cavaliers' prowess with the sword and lance from horseback. However, whether tent pegging developed cavaliers' generic skills or prepared them for specific combat situations is shrouded in anecdote and national chauvinism.

The most widely accepted theory is that the game originated in medieval India as a training tool for cavaliers facing war elephants. A cavalier able to precisely stab the highly sensitive flesh behind an elephant's toenail would cause the enemy elephant to rear, unseat his mahout, and possibly run amok, breaking ranks and trampling infantry.

The term "tent pegging" is, however, certainly related to the idea that cavaliers mounting a surprise pre-dawn raid on an enemy camp could use the game's skills to sever or uproot tent pegs, thus collapsing the tents on their sleeping occupants and sowing havoc and terror in the camp. However, there are few reliable accounts of a cavalry squadron ever employing such tactics.

Because the specific game of tent pegging is the most popular equestrian skill-at-arms game, the entire class of sports became known as tent pegging during the twilight of cavalry in the twentieth century.

Contemporary sport

Today, tent pegging is practised around the world, but is especially popular in Australia, India, Israel, Oman, Pakistan, South Africa, and the United Kingdom. The Olympic Council of Asia included tent pegging as an official sport in 1982, and the International Federation for Equestrian Sports recognised it as an official equestrian discipline in 2004.

From the results of the 2008 International Tent Pegging Championships, the world's three leading national teams are currently Canada, India, and Oman.

While members of cavalry regiments and mounted police forces still dominate world-class tent pegging, the sport is being increasingly embraced by civilian riders.

New and emerging national tent pegging associations have helped spread the sport's popularity. The Australian Royal Adelaide Show, the British Tent Pegging Association, and the United States Cavalry Association now hold annual national championships and demonstrations in their respective countries.

The pre-eminent tent pegging games remain centred in Asia and the Middle East, with the International Tent Pegging Championships and the continental Asian Games traditionally enjoying the highest number of competitors and participating states.

Source (edited): "http://en.wikipedia.org/wiki/Tent_pegging"

2010 Longines Royal International Horse Show

The **2010 Longines Royal International Horse Show** was the 2010 edition of the Royal International Horse Show, the British official show jumping horse show at All England Jumping Course at Hickstead. It was held as CSIO 5* and CDI 5*.

The 2010 edition of the Longines Royal International Horse Show was held between July 29, 2010 and August 1, 2010.

FEI Nations Cup of Great Britain

The 2010 FEI Nations Cup of the United Kingdom is part of the 2010 Longines Royal International Horse Show. It was the seventh competition of the 2010 Meydan FEI Nations Cup.

The 2010 FEI Nations Cup of the United Kingdom was held at Friday, July 30, 2010 at 1:45 pm. The competing teams were: France, the United States of America, Germany, Switzerland, the Netherlands, Ireland, Sweden, Great Britain and Spain (the team of Poland did not start in this competition).

The competition was a show jumping competition with two rounds and optionally one jump-off. The height of the fences were up to 1.60 meters. Eight of ten (here: eight of nine) teams are allowed to start in the second round.

The competition was endowed with

200,000 €.
(grey penalties points do not count for the team result)

Grand Prix Spécial (B-Final)

The 2010 Longines Royal International Horse Show was the venue of the third competition of the World Dressage Masters (WDM) - rider ranking, season 2010/2011.

All competitors starts first in the Grand Prix de Dressage at Thursday. The eight best-placed competitors of the Grand Prix de Dressage are allowed to start in the A-Final (the Grand Prix Freestyle). It some of best-placed competitors want to start in the B-Final, the same number of competitors, who are placed after the best-placed competitors, move up in the A-Final.

The B-Final of the World Dressage Masters competitions at 2010 Longines Royal International Horse Show was held at Sunday, August 1, 2010. It was endowed with 30,000 €. The B-Final was held as Grand Prix Spécial, the competition with the highest definite level of dressage competitions.
(top 3 of 10 competitors)

Grand Prix Freestyle (A-Final)

The Grand Prix Freestyle (or Grand Prix Kür) was the A-Final of the World Dressage Masters competitions at 2010 Longines Royal International Horse Show (see also Grand Prix Spécial).

A Grand Prix Freestyle was a Freestyle dressage competition. The level of this competition is at least the level of a Grand Prix de Dressage, but it can be higher than the level of a Grand Prix Spécial.

The Grand Prix Freestyle at 2010 Longines Royal International Horse Show was held at Sunday, August 1, 2010 after the Grand Prix Spécial. It was endowed with 60,000 €.
(top 5 of 8 competitors)

The Longines King Georges V Gold Cup

The King Georges V Gold Cup, the Show jumping Grand Prix of the 2010 Longines Royal International Horse Show, was the mayor show jumping competition at this event. The sponsor of this competition is Longines. It was held at Sunday, August 1, 2010 at 2:45 pm. The competition was a show jumping competition with one round and one jump-off, the height of the fences were up to 1.60 meters.

It was endowed with 200,000 £.
(Top 5 of 44 Competitors)
Source (edited): "http://en.wikipedia.org/wiki/2010_Longines_Royal_International_Horse_Show"

Royal International Horse Show

The **Royal International Horse Show** is the official horse show of the British Horse Society and consists of both showing and showjumping events. The event is held during July each year at the All England Jumping Course at Hickstead. The event is currently title sponsored by Longines, making it the **Longines Royal International Horse Show**.

The show is the oldest horse show in Britain, having started in 1907.

History

The first Royal International Horse Show was held at London Olympia in 1907, hosted by the Institute of the Horse and Pony Club, which would later become the British Horse Society. Having also been held at Wembley Stadium and the National Exhibition Centre in Birmingham, the show moved to the All England Jumping Course at Hickstead in 1992.
Source (edited): "http://en.wikipedia.org/wiki/Royal_International_Horse_Show"